# Air Fryer Cookbook

## Easy to Make Air Fryer Recipes for Every Taste!

© **Copyright 2016 Simon Donovan - All rights reserved.**

This document is geared towards providing exact and reliable information in regards to the topic and issue covered. The publication is sold with the idea that the publisher is not required to render accounting, officially permitted, or otherwise, qualified services. If advice is necessary, legal or professional, a practiced individual in the profession should be ordered.

- From a Declaration of Principles which was accepted and approved equally by a Committee of the American Bar Association and a Committee of Publishers and Associations.

In no way is it legal to reproduce, duplicate, or transmit any part of this document in either electronic means or in printed format. Recording of this publication is strictly prohibited and any storage of this document is not allowed unless with written permission from the publisher. All rights reserved.

The information provided herein is stated to be truthful and consistent, in that any liability, in terms of inattention or otherwise, by any usage or abuse of any policies, processes, or directions contained within is the solitary and utter responsibility of the recipient reader. Under no circumstances will any legal responsibility or blame be held against the publisher for any reparation, damages, or monetary loss due to the information herein, either directly or indirectly.

Respective authors own all copyrights not held by the publisher.

The information herein is offered for informational purposes solely, and is universal as so. The presentation of the information is without contract or any type of guarantee assurance.

The trademarks that are used are without any consent, and the publication of the trademark is without permission or backing by the trademark owner. All trademarks and brands within this book are for clarifying purposes only and are the owned by the owners themselves, not affiliated with this document.

# Table of Contents

Introduction .................................................................... 1

Chapter 1: Your Air Fryer ............................................... 2

Chapter 2: Appetizers ..................................................... 5

Chapter 3: Entrées ........................................................ 25

Chapter 4: Desserts ...................................................... 41

Chapter 5: Snacks ......................................................... 57

Conclusion .................................................................... 65

# Introduction

Thank you for purchasing *Air Fryer Cookbook: Easy to Make Air Fryer Recipes for Every Taste!* This book is the perfect companion book for learning about your air fryer and making the most of it. Throughout this book you will learn how to maximize the benefits of your air fryer, as well as how to make some incredibly delicious, and simple, air fryer recipes.

Air fryers are an incredible invention that has allowed for people to enjoy their favorite fried foods without compromising their health. When you choose to air fry your meals, you still get the crunchy, scrumptious taste but you don't face any of the health risks that come with eating too much fried food. It is also easy to do, and reduces the risk of any burns from cooking with burning hot oil.

You might be surprised to find out just how much your air fryer can do. In this book, we are going to discover all of the amazing benefits of these amazing countertop appliances. By the end, you will have mastered all of the basics of your air fryer and will be well on your way to using it to its full potential.

# Chapter 1: Your Air Fryer

Air fryers are currently one of the most popular small appliances to own. This simple countertop appliance fries your food without any oil, meaning you are eating healthier food with the same great taste. Air fryers work by rapidly circulating super-hot air (up to 200 degrees Celsius) around your food, causing it to cook to the same crispness as oil frying does. Air fryers make the perfect fried food that is browned and crisped to perfection and featuring up to 80 percent less fat compared to traditional frying and cooking methods.

Each individual air fryer will come with a set of instructions on how that model is to be used. They all generally work in the same way, but to be safe, it is best that you follow the instructions set for your specific model. Below, we have curated a list of tips to help you become an air frying pro in no time. These tips are gathered from various air frying pros, and work across all air fryers.

**Shake It Up**
While you are cooking with your air fryer, you should make sure you regularly open up the air fryer and give the basket a good shake. You should also rotate the foods inside every five to ten minutes. Doing this prevents your food from cooking unevenly, or sticking together or to your air fryer basket.

**Spray Your Food**
Even though this air fryer doesn't require heaps of oil to work, it is still a good idea to use a high quality cooking oil to prevent sticking. When preparing to fry in your air fryer, you can gently

spray them with a good cooking spray and then proceed to air fry as normal. This can prevent pieces from sticking together or to your air frying appliance.

## Don't Overcrowd the Fryer

It is a good idea to break larger recipes down into multiple batches. You should keep from overcrowding your air fryer, as this will end with poor results. The air needs to be able to circulate your food efficiently in order to cook it properly.

## Dry Your Foods First

If the foods you are preparing to fry are fairly moist, such as marinated foods or naturally wet vegetables like potatoes, you should pat them dry before frying them. This prevents excess smoke and splatters. For a quick drying method, you can try using a salad spinner to spin your ingredients dry. You should also keep the basket dry. If you are cooking high-fat foods that leak fat into the basket, you should periodically empty it and dry it out before proceeding to the next batch.

## Take It for A Test Drive

While it might be an air fryer, it doesn't mean you can't do a bunch of other amazing things with it. Your air fryer can be used to roast, grill, and even bake! In fact, we have dedicated an entire dessert section in this book towards teaching you how to properly bake with your air fryer.

## Start with The Slow Stuff

When you are cooking larger things with your air fryer, you will want to start with the slower cooking ingredients, first. It is completely okay to open the air fryer during the cooking process, so don't worry about adding quicker cooking ingredients later on, like halfway through, cooking your dish. Make sure you time everything so it is all done at the same time and nothing gets over – or under – cooked.

## Never Wash in the Dishwasher

You should never wash your air fryer in the dishwasher. While most will advertise that they are dishwasher safe, using the dishwasher can be harsh on the plastics in your unit. Instead, wash your air fryer by hand. It will increase the longevity of it and keep you from having to replace parts, or the entire unit, any time soon.

There are many amazing things you can do with your air fryer. They are phenomenal appliances that became extremely popular in 2010. Since then, their sales have sky rocketed and they can now be found in thousands of kitchens across the world. It is for good reason, too. Air fryers are healthier frying options that allow us to keep eating our favorite dishes without worrying about having to pay with our health. Air fryers are brilliant small appliances, and you will definitely fall in love with yours in no time.

# Chapter 2: Appetizers

These amazing appetizers are simple to make and absolutely delicious. They will make a wonderful, healthy addition to any of your favorite meals. You and your family will be sure to love these appetizers!

**Fried Broccoli**

This is a delicious, crispy recipe that is a wonderful addition to any meal. Pair it with a tasty sauce of your choice and you will definitely be loving your healthy appetizer.

This recipe takes 10 minutes to prepare, 20 minutes to cook and makes 4 servings of 1 cup each.

Fat 4.6 grams
Calories 96

*Ingredients:*
- 1 Head Broccoli, large
- 1/2 Lemon, juiced
- 3 Cloves Garlic, minced
- 1 tablespoon Duck Fat, or coconut oil
- 1 tablespoon Sesame Seeds, white
- 2 teaspoons Maggi sauce, or other seasonings to taste

*Instructions:*
1. Thoroughly wash head of broccoli and then chop into bite-sized pieces. Pat pieces dry and set them aside
2. Peel garlic, mince and set aside
3. In your air fryer basket, combine duck fat (or coconut oil) with lemon juice and Maggi sauce. Heat the concoction for 2 minutes at 160C (320F) and stir.

4. Add garlic and broccoli, combine and cook for 13 minutes.
5. Sprinkle white sesame seeds over broccoli and cook for a final 5 minutes, just to toast the sesame seeds.
6. Serve hot

## Fried Mushrooms

These fried mushrooms are an amazing appetizer to be enjoyed with any meal. You can add them to a dish as a topping, such as burgers, or you can eat them on their own. They are a savory way to enjoy mushrooms with your favorite meal.

*This recipe takes 10 minutes to prepare, 30 minutes to cook and makes 4 servings of 1 cup each.*

*Fat 3.9 grams*
*Calories 92*

*Ingredients:*
- 2 Pounds Button Mushrooms
- 3 Tablespoons White or French Vermouth (optional)
- 1 Tablespoon Duck Fat, or coconut oil
- 2 Teaspoon Herbs of Your Choice
- ½ Teaspoon Garlic Powder

*Instructions:*
1. Thoroughly wash your mushrooms and then dry them. Cut them into quarters and set them aside.
2. Heat your air fryer to 160C (320F) and add the following ingredients to the basket: duck fat (or coconut oil), garlic powder, and herbs. Warm the ingredients for 2 minutes, stir and then add the mushrooms.
3. Cook the mushrooms for 25 minutes, stirring periodically.
4. Add white vermouth, stir and cook for another 5 minutes.
5. Serve hot.

# Grilled Endive Marinated in Curried Yogurt

This endive appetizer is coated with a delicious yogurt curry. It is healthy, tasty, and serves a wonderful authentic flavor along any dish. You can eat these on their own, or put them over top of a bowl of rice to enjoy as a meal all on their own.

*This recipe takes 10 minutes to prepare, 10 minutes to cook and makes 6 servings of 2 pieces each.*

*Fat 1.3 grams*
*Calories 106*

*Ingredients:*
- 6 Heads Endive
- 1/2 Cup Yogurt, plain and fat-free
- 3 Tablespoons Lemon Juice
- 1 Teaspoon Garlic Powder (or 2 minced cloves of garlic)
- 1/2 Teaspoon Curry Powder
- Salt and Ground Black Pepper to Taste

*Instructions:*
1. Thoroughly wash endives, then halve them lengthwise through the root end. Set the endives aside.
2. In a bowl, combine yogurt, lemon juice, garlic powder (or mince), curry powder, salt and pepper. If you need the marinated thinner, add more lemon juice.
3. Take the endive halves and either toss them in the marinade, or generously brush them with it.
4. Cover the pieces and let them marinade for at least 30 minutes, or as long as a day.
5. Preheat air fryer to 160C (320F) and cook the endives for 10 minutes
6. Serve hot

## Grilled Tomatoes

Tomatoes are a healthy, flavorful fruit. These grilled tomatoes are scrumptious, savory, and full of flavor. You can eat them as is, or put them over top of another one of your favorite dishes. These tomatoes can be coated with any number of herbs to enhance the flavor, or you can serve them as is.

*This recipe takes 5 minutes to prepare, 20 minutes to cook and makes 2 servings of 2 pieces each.*

*Fat 0.8 grams*
*Calories 27*

*Ingredients:*
- 2 Tomatoes, medium to large
- Herbs of Choice, to taste
- Pepper, to taste
- High Quality Cooking Spray

*Instructions:*
1. Thoroughly wash tomatoes, pat them dry, and halve them. Turn them over so the skin is up, and lightly spray them with a quick spray of cooking oil.
2. Turn halves cut side up and spray again, lightly with one quick spray.
3. Sprinkle the halves with your choice of herbs and some black pepper. (Ideal herbs: oregano, basil, parsley, rosemary, thyme, sage, etc.)
4. Place halves into the tray of your air fryer
5. Cook for 20 minutes at 160C (320F).
6. After 20 minutes, check to see if they are done. If not, you can add an extra 5 minutes on the cook time until they are cooked to your desired doneness. Larger tomatoes will need more cook time.
7. Serve hot.

# Heritage Carrots and Rhubarb

These carrots and rhubarb are a sweet, flavorful dish. Topped with walnuts, this appetizer is a delicious meal that offers a wonderful, healthy side to any entrée you may serve up.

*This recipe takes 10 minutes to prepare, 25 minutes to cook and makes 4 servings of 1/2 cup each.*

*Fat 10.1 grams*
*Calories 182*

*Ingredients:*
- 1 Pound Heritage Carrots
- 1 Pound Rhubarb
- 1 Orange, medium
- 1/2 Cup Walnuts, halved
- 2 Teaspoons Walnut Oil
- 1/2 Teaspoon Stevia (or a few drops of stevia extract)

*Instructions:*
1. Thoroughly wash carrots, and pat them dry. Cut them into 1 inch pieces and place them in the air fryer basket with walnut oil.
2. Heat fryer to 160C (320F) and cook the carrots for about 20 minutes.
3. In the meantime, thoroughly wash the rhubarb and cut it into 1/2 inch pieces. Set aside.
4. Roughly chop the walnuts, and set aside.
5. Thoroughly wash the orange, zest it and then set the zest aside. Peel and section the rest of the orange, and set the sections aside.
6. After cooking the carrots for 20 minutes, add the rhubarb, walnuts and stevia and cook it for another 5 minutes.
7. Stir in 2 tablespoons of orange zest, and add the peeled sections of the orange to the dish.
8. Serve immediately.

## Jalapeno Poppers

These jalapeno poppers are a wonderful way to enjoy a favorite classic. They can be served with nearly any sauce, and make a great appetizer or snack. They are wonderful as a side to any meal, or to have served up on game night or any other hosting night.

*This recipe takes 20 minutes to prepare, 10 minutes to cook and makes 1 servings of 2 pieces each.*

*Fat 1.6 grams*
*Calories 166*

*Ingredients:*
- 1 Spring Roll Wrapper
- 2 Jalapeno Peppers, medium
- 1 Ounce Cheddar Cheese, low fat
- 1 Tablespoon Liquid Egg Mixture
- High Quality Cooking Spray

*Instructions:*
1. Wear gloves when working with jalapeno peppers to prevent spreading the oils to your eyes or other areas where it could cause burning.
2. Chop the stem end off of the jalapenos, slice them lengthwise and trim out the innards. Rinse under water if necessary to remove stubborn seeds. If wet, pat dry and set aside, keeping matching halves together.
3. Cut cheddar cheese into two 1/2 ounce strips.
4. Take a sheet of spring roll wrapper and cut it in half. Brush each half of the wrapper with the liquid egg mixture, focusing on the edges in particular.
5. In one corner of the spring roll wrapper halve, place the jalapeno cut side up. Fill the jalapeno with a cheddar cheese strip and top it with the remaining jalapeno halve (keeping both halves of the same jalapenos together.)

6. Folding in the edges, roll the jalapeno popper up in the spring roll wrapper.
7. When the popper is wrapped, make sure the wrapper is tight and give the entire popper a light brush with liquid egg mixture.
8. After you have assembled both of the jalapeno poppers, lay them down and lightly spray them with high quality cooking spray. Turn poppers over and spray the other side.
9. Place your poppers in your air fryer basket and cook for 10 minutes at 160C (320F). If you are making enough for multiple servings, you can comfortably fit about 8 in your air fryer basket at a time. (That is enough to serve 4 people.)
10. If they aren't golden brown enough for your taste, let them cook for another minute or two.
11. Serve poppers immediately as is, or with a marinara dipping sauce.

## Maple Glazed Beets

These sweetly glazed beets are a flavorful way to enjoy a deliciously healthy root vegetable. The maple topping adds heaps of flavor to an already satisfying dish of beets. This recipe serves wonderfully alongside any of your favorite fall recipes.

*This recipe takes 10 minutes to prepare, 50 minutes to cook and makes 8 servings of 1/2 cup each.*

*Fat 1.7 grams*
*Calories 68*

*Ingredients:*
- 3.5 Pounds Beetroots
- 4 Tablespoons Maple Syrup
- 1 Tablespoon Duck Fat, or coconut oil

*Instructions:*
1. Gently but thoroughly wash the beets, then peel them. Chop them into 1 inch pieces and set them aside.
2. Put the duck fat or coconut oil in the air fryer and heat for 1 minute at 160C (320F) until melted.
3. Add the beet cubes to the air fryer basket
4. Cook for 40 minutes
5. Cover the beetroots in half of the maple syrup and cook for an additional 10 minutes, or until the beets are fork tender.
6. When the beets are done to your desire, toss them with the remaining half of the maple syrup.
7. Serve immediately.

## Maple Roasted Parsnip

This maple roasted parsnip recipe is sweet, flavorful and have an addicting texture. They are wonderful served next to any of your favorite fall recipes or meat dishes.

*This recipe takes 10 minutes to prepare, 45 minutes to cook and makes 5 servings of 1 cup each.*

*Fat 3.1 grams*
*Calories 260*

Ingredients:
- 2 Pounds Parsnips (about 6 large parsnips)
- 2 Tablespoons Maple Syrup
- 1 Tablespoon Duck Fat, or coconut oil
- 1 Tablespoon Parsley, dried flakes

Instructions:
1. Put the duck fat or coconut oil in your air fryer and heat for 2 minutes at 160C (320F) until melted.
2. Thoroughly wash your parsnips and peel them, then cut into 1 inch cubes. Put the parsnip cubes into the melted duck fat (or coconut oil).
3. Cook the parsnip cubes for 40 minutes, tossing them periodically. Test for fork tenderness and add a few minutes to the cook time if necessary.
4. In the final five minutes of cooking, sprinkle the parsnips with parsley and maple syrup.
5. Serve immediately.

## Roasted Orange Carrots

This citrusy spin on a favorite classic of roasted carrots is a wonderful way to add excitement to any meal. These carrots are roasted in your air fryer, and then flavored with orange juice to fill them with a tasty, unique flavor that will make your taste buds jump with joy.

*This recipe takes 10 minutes to prepare, 25 minutes to cook and makes 4 servings of 3/4 cup each.*

*Fat 2.9 grams*
*Calories 84*

*Ingredients:*
- 1 Pound Carrots
- 4 Tablespoons Orange Juice, no pulp
- 2 Teaspoons Extra Virgin Olive Oil
- 1 Teaspoon Herbes De Provence, or herbs of choice

*Instructions:*
1. Thoroughly wash the carrots and cut them into 1 inch cubes. Do not peel them.
2. Preheat your air fryer to 160C (320F)
3. Put the carrot chunks into your air fryer basket, add the herbs and then coat with oil. (Always add oil after herbs so the herbs are wet and don't get blown around the air fryer.)
4. Roast the mixture for 20 minutes.
5. After 20 minutes, add the orange juice and continue roasting for an additional 5 minutes.
6. Serve hot.

# Roasted Eggplant

Eggplants are an extremely healthy vegetable. These roasted eggplants feature a delicious concoction of garlic powder, Maggi sauce and a few other seasonings to create a wild flavor that will have you craving more. They are excellent alongside any of your favorite dishes, especially those that star meat or other fall inspired dishes.

*This recipe takes 15 minutes to prepare, 25 minutes to cook and makes 6 servings of 1/2 cup each.*

*Fat 3.4 grams*
*Calories 67*

*Ingredients:*
- 3 Eggplants, medium
- 1/2 Lemon, juiced
- 1 Tablespoon Duck Fat, or coconut oil
- 1 Tablespoon Maggi Sauce
- 3 Teaspoons Za'atar
- 1 Teaspoon Sumac
- 1 Teaspoon Garlic Powder
- 1 Teaspoon Onion Powder
- 1 Teaspoon Extra Virgin Olive Oil
- 2 Bay Leaves

*Instructions:*
Thoroughly wash your eggplants and pat them dry. Destem the eggplants, then cut them into 1 inch cubes. Set the cubes aside.
In your air fryer basket, combine duck fat (or coconut oil), maggi sauce, za'atar, onion powder, garlic powder, sumac and bay leaves.

Cook the ingredients for 2 minutes at 160C (320F) until melted. Stir together.

Add the eggplant into the air fryer basket.

Cook the eggplant for 25 minutes.

In a large mixing bowl, combine the lemon juice and extra virgin olive oil. Stir in the cooked eggplant and toss until they are evenly coated.

Serve immediately with an optional garnish of grated parmesan or fresh chopped basil.

## Roasted Peppers

Roasted peppers are a soft dish that is rich with flavor. These peppers are coated with Maggi sauce to enhance the flavor and make them extra tasty. You will love eating these with any of your favorite dishes.

*This recipe takes 15 minutes to prepare, 25 minutes to cook and makes 4 servings of 3/4 cup each.*

*Fat 1.9 grams*
*Calories 63*

Ingredients:
- 12 Bell Peppers, medium
- 1 Sweet Onion, small
- 1 Tablespoon Maggi Sauce
- 1 Tablespoon Extra Virgin Olive Oil

Instructions:
1. Heat your air fryer to 160C (320F) and warm the extra virgin olive oil and Maggi sauce together.
2. Peel the onion, chop it into 1 inch slices, and put it in the warmed oil mixture in the air fyer.
3. Wash the peppers, destem them, cut them into 1 inch pieces, and clean out the seeds. If you need to, rinse away the tough seeds and pat the peppers dry. Add them to the air fryer.
4. Cook them for about 25 minutes, give or take depending on what your preferred doneness is.

## Roasted Potatoes

Having a side of roasted potatoes is a classic. They go great with fish, chicken, steak, or any other meat-oriented dish. They can be seasoned with any herbs you desire to create your choice of flavor, or left unseasoned to be enjoyed as is. Either way, you will love the crunchy outer texture wrapped around a delicious, soft filling.

*This recipe takes 5 minutes to prepare, 40 minutes to cook and makes 4 servings of 1 cup each.*

*Fat 3.1 grams*
*Calories 260*

*Ingredients:*
- 2 ¾ Pound Potatoes (about 2 large Russet Potatoes)
- 1 Teaspoon Extra Virgin Olive Oil (or coconut oil)
- Herbs of Choice, to taste

*Instructions:*
1. Thoroughly wash the potatoes and cut them into 1 inch cubes. Don't peel them beforehand.
2. In a medium bowl, toss together your potato cubes and extra virgin olive oil until the cubes are evenly coated.
3. Cook your potato cubes in the air fryer at 160C (320F) for 25 minutes. Don't preheat your air fryer, you don't need to.
4. When they're done, toss them gently and then raise the temperature to 180C (350F) and cook them for another 7 minutes.
5. Finally, remove them from the bowl and toss them in a medium bowl with your choice of herbs.
6. Serve hot. Reheat in air fryer as needed.

## Sweet Potato Fries

These sweet potato fries are a delicious spin on standard French fries. They are extra healthy, rich with flavor and pair great with a chipotle mayo sauce. These are easy to make, require few ingredients, and will enhance any dish you serve them with.

*This recipe takes 5 minutes to prepare, 30 minutes to cook and makes 5 servings of 1 cup each.*

*Fat 3.1 grams*
*Calories 260*

*Ingredients:*
- 2 Sweet Potatoes, large
- 1 Tablespoon Extra Virgin Olive Oil

*Instructions:*
1. Wash and peel the sweet potatoes
2. Chop into shoestring fries and place into a large bowl
3. Using clean hands, add the oil and then toss the fries thoroughly. Make sure all of the fries are thoroughly coated so they don't stick to each other, and they cook evenly.
4. Set your air fryer to 160C (320F), place sweet potatoes in the air fryer basket and fry them for 15 minutes. Toss them once about halfway through the cooking process.
5. After 15 minutes, give the fries a really thorough toss.
6. Raise the air fryer temperature to 180C (350F) and cook sweet potato fries for another 5 minutes.
7. Thoroughly toss your sweet potato fries, and then let them fry for another 5 minutes.
8. Serve your fries immediately, straight out of the air fryer.

## Tofu

Tofu is a healthy variety to meat options. While it is a popular choice among vegetarians, it can also be thoroughly enjoyed by just about anyone. Tofu has a soft, adaptive flavor that can be seasoned to create any taste. When it is fried, it creates a scrumptious, crispy outer layer while still keeping its deliciously soft interior. This tofu is easy to make, features an authentic oriental flavor and will definitely make you fall in love with air fried tofu.

*This recipe takes 10 minutes to prepare, 20 minutes to cook and makes 4 servings of 1/2 cup each.*

*Fat 2.2 grams*
*Calories 27*

*Ingredients:*
- 1x 12oz Package Tofu, low-fat and extra firm
- 2 Tablespoons Soy Sauce, low-sodium
- 2 Tablespoons Fish Sauce
- 1 Tablespoon Coriander Paste
- 1 Teaspoon Sesame Oil
- 1 Teaspoon Duck Fat (or coconut oil)
- 1 Teaspoon Maggi Sauce

*Instructions:*
1. Drain the package of tofu and then cut the contents into 1 inch cubes. Place them out on a paper towel lined plate evenly, and in a single layer. Cover them with more paper towel, put another plate on top and place something on it to weigh it down. This will thoroughly dry your tofu out. You can change the paper towel once or twice to get it extra dry. Ideally you should dry tofu for at least 30 minutes before cooking with it, though you can go as long as overnight if you have the time.

2. In a medium bowl, mix together: sesame oil, Maggi sauce, coriander paste, fish sauce, and soy sauce. Blend thoroughly to make your marinade.
3. Place your dried tofu into the marinade bowl and mix thoroughly so they are evenly coated. Let the cubes marinate for about 30 minutes, or longer if possible. Toss the cubes a few times while marinating to keep them evenly coated and make sure they all get a strong dose of flavor. If the marinade is too thick and isn't coating well, add an additional squirt of fish sauce or soy sauce to thin it out and help it spread easier.
4. Heat your air fryer to 180C (350F) and let your duck fat or coconut oil melt for about 2 minutes. Add the tofu cubes to the basket and let them cook for about 20 minutes. If you prefer them extra crispy, you can cook them for as long as 30 minutes. Turn the cubes or shake the basket every 10 minutes to keep them frying evenly and thoroughly.
5. Serve hot with your choice of dipping sauce.

## Zucchini Wedges

These breaded zucchini wedges are a tasty alternative to traditional French fries. They are healthy, have a crunchy exterior, and are full of flavor. You can serve them with just about any dipping sauce from ketchup to plain or flavored mayo, and they will pair perfectly. They are a wonderful, healthy alternative that will compliment any dish you serve them with.

*This recipe takes 10 minutes to prepare, 35 minutes to cook and makes 4 servings of 8 pieces each.*

*Fat 1.7 grams*
*Calories 76*

Ingredients:
- 2 Zucchinis, medium and fully ripe
- ½ Cup Panko Bread Crumbs, or anything else you have on hand
- ¼ Cup Egg Whites (approximately 2 egg whites)
- ¼ Cup Parmesan Cheese, grated
- ¼ Teaspoon Cayenne Pepper
- ¼ Teaspoon Basil
- ¼ Teaspoon Oregano
- High Quality Cooking Spray

Instructions:
1. In a medium bowl, combine panko bread crumbs, parmesan cheese, cayenne pepper, basil, and oregano. Mix until well blended and then set aside.
2. Thoroughly wash your zucchinis, and pat them dry. Don't peel them.
3. Cut the zucchini in half crosswise and then cut it into wedges no more than ½ inch thick.
4. Spray the air fryer basket with a high quality cooking spray.

5. In a shallow bowl or dish, lightly beat egg whites. Then, in another shallow dish, place a small portion of your breadcrumb mix. (Only work with a small portion at a time so it doesn't become drenched with egg whites and then unusable.)
6. With each wedge, dip the zucchini into the egg white and then thoroughly coat it with the bread crumbs, pressing them down so they stay in place. Put your zucchini wedges into the air fryer pan. Do not overfill your air fryer pan, cook in a single layer in multiple batches if necessary.
7. Once your basket is full, lightly spray the wedges with your high quality cooking spray. Heat the air fryer to 180C (350F) and cook the wedges for about 7 minutes and then turn them over. Cook them for an additional 7 minutes and then remove them from the air fryer. Place the finished wedges in a serving dish that can be kept warm while you complete additional batches.
8. Serve the wedges hot with your choice of dipping sauce.

# Chapter 3: Entrées

These hearty entrées are so good that no one will ever guess that they were so easy to make! They are completed right in your air fryer and require little effort. Each dish is healthy, filling and pairs phenomenally with one of our many appetizers featured in this cook book. You will be sure to enjoy our classics as well as our original recipes, and the only difference you'll notice is how much better they are!

**Burgers**
These hearty burgers are seasoned to perfection. Their rich flavor makes them a delicious main course for any dinner. They are easy to make, require little effort to prepare, and will leave you wanting more. You will never want to eat out again once you learn to make these tasty burgers right in your own kitchen with your air fryer!

*This recipe takes 10 minutes to prepare, 10 minutes to cook and makes 4 servings of 1 piece each.*

*Fat 4.6 grams*
*Calories 148*

Ingredients:
- 1 Pound Ground Beef, extra-lean, uncooked
- 1 Tablespoon Worcestershire Sauce
- 1 Teaspoon Maggi Sauce
- 1 Teaspoon Parsley, dried flakes
- ½ Teaspoon Garlic Powder
- ½ Teaspoon Onion Powder
- ½ Teaspoon Oregano, dried

- A Few Drops of Liquid Smoke
- Salt and Ground Black Pepper to Taste
- High Quality Cooking Spray

*Instructions:*
1. In a small bowl, combine Worcestershire sauce, Maggi sauce, liquid smoke, garlic powder, onion powder, salt and ground black pepper, oregano, and parsley. Blend together until it is thoroughly mixed.
2. Place the ground beef in a large glass bowl, and add the seasoning mixture to it.
3. Combine the two evenly without overmixing the meat. (Working the meat too much can lead to a tough patty.)
4. Take the beef and divide it into four even sections, and shape it into four patties. Using your thumb, press a small indentation in the middle of each patty. This keeps them from bunching up and helps them cook more evenly.
5. Place the patties in the air fryer basket and put the heat to 180C (350F).
6. Cook the burgers for 10 minutes if they're medium, or longer if they're not done enough for you. You do not need to flip the patties during the cooking process.
7. Serve hot on a bun with any toppings and sides you desire.

# Fried "Faux" Rice

This "faux" rice dish is actually made from cauliflower! It is delicious, healthy, and you can eat as much as you desire without compromising on your health. This dish can be flavored in any way you desire, using any number of herbs, vegetables, or sauces. It is a wonderful main dish to be enjoyed in any way you desire.

*This recipe takes 20 minutes to prepare, 40 minutes to cook and makes 8 servings of 1 cup each.*

*Fat 3.9 grams*
*Calories 133*

*Ingredients:*
- 1 Head of Cauliflower, medium to large
- ½ Lemon, juiced
- 4 Garlic Cloves, minced
- 2 Cans Mushrooms, 8oz each
- 1 Can Water Chestnuts, 8oz
- ¾ Cup Peas
- ½ Cup Egg Substitute, or one egg beat together
- 4 Tablespoons Soy Sauce
- 1 Tablespoon Peanut Oil
- 1 Tablespoon Sesame Oil
- 1 Tablespoon Ginger, fresh and minced
- High Quality Cooking Spray

*Instructions:*
1. In a bowl, combine: sesame oil, peanut oil, soy sauce, minced garlic, minced ginger, and lemon juice. Mix together until thoroughly blended.
2. Peel the cauliflower and thoroughly wash it. Then, cut the head into smaller florets. Don't leave the florets too large.
3. In a food processor, process the florets a few at a time. Process them until they are just broken down to about the size of rice

grains. Empty into your air fryer basket and continue until all of the cauliflower has been processed.
4. Completely drain the water chestnut can and then chop them coarsely. Add them to the cauliflower in the air fryer basket.
5. Turn the air fryer on to 180C (350F) and cook for 20 minutes.
6. After the cauliflower has cooked for 20 minutes, drain the mushrooms and add them, as well as the peas, to the cauliflower. Cook the mixture for an additional 15 minutes.
7. In a frying pan, lightly spray it with high quality cooking spray. Then, make a solid omelet with the egg substitute or the beaten egg. Place the omelet on a cutting board and chop it up.
8. When the cauliflower concoction is done cooking for the additional 15 minutes, add the egg and cook it for a final 5 minutes.
9. Serve immediately.

# Green Curry Noodles

These delicious green curry noodles are made with healthy Shirataki noodles. It is authentic, healthy, and a delicious recipe that can be made in your air fryer on your counter top. You will absolutely love this curry recipe.

*This recipe takes 1 hour 15 minutes to prepare, 25 minutes to cook and makes 6 servings of ¾ cup each.*

*Fat 6.1 grams*
*Calories 271*

*Ingredients:*
- 2 Pounds Shirataki Noodles
- 12 oz Tofu, extra firm
- 12 oz Napa Cabbage
- 5 oz Snow Peas
- 1 Red Pepper, medium and thinly sliced
- 1 Green Pepper, medium and thinly sliced
- 2 Carrots, medium and shredded
- 4 Spring Onions, finely chopped
- 12 Shrimp, large and cooked
- ¼ Pound Mushrooms, thinly sliced
- 1 Cup Water Chestnuts, sliced
- 6 Tablespoons Thai Green Curry Paste
- 6 Tablespoons Soy Sauce, low-sodium
- 4 Tablespoons Rice Vinegar
- 3 Tablespoons Lime Juice
- 1 ½ Tablespoons Fish Sauce, thai
- 2 Teaspoons Lemon Grass Paste
- 1 Teaspoon Sesame Oil
- 1 Teaspoon Coriander Paste
- ½ Teaspoon Garlic Powder
- High Quality Cooking Spray

*Instructions:*
1. Drain your tofu, cut it into ½ inch cubes and place it on a paper towel covered plate in a single layer. Cover the tofu with more paper towel, place another plate on top and add a weight on top. Let the tofu dry thoroughly while you complete the next steps.
2. Drain your Shirataki Noodles if they were packaged in water, through a sieve. Rinse them thoroughly with fresh water, then place them in a bowl with 2 cups of boiling water from a kettle. Add 1 tablespoon of soy sauce, stir and set aside.
3. In a medium bowl, make a marinade by combining: 3 tablespoons of soy sauce (save 2 tablespoons for later), sesame oil, fish sauce and garlic powder.
4. Take your dried tofu, put it in the bowl with the marinade and toss the two together until the tofu is evenly coated. Set it aside to marinate while you prepare the next steps. Toss the tofu every now and again to recoat it.
5. Prepare your veggies for the stir fry from the snow peas, red pepper, green pepper, mushrooms, and water chestnuts. Set the mixture aside for now.
6. In a small bowl, mix together the coriander paste, lime juice, lemon grass paste, and 4 tablespoons of the Thai green curry paste (saving the additional 2 tablespoons for later), and 2 tablespoons of the rice vinegar (saving the additional 2 tablespoons for later.) Blend until thoroughly combined and then set aside.
7. Make a base of fresh vegetables by combining the shredded cabbage, shredded carrot and finely chopped spring onions together. Set this mixture aside.
8. Lightly spray the basket of your air fryer with high quality cooking spray, then place the tofu in the basket. Spray the tofu lightly with some of the cooking spray.
9. Cook the tofu for about 12-13 minutes at 180C (350F)
10. When the tofu cubes are done, do the same with the shrimp. Remove the two, set them aside and cover them to keep them warm.
11. Make your stir-fry sauce by covering the left-over tofu marinade, 2 tablespoons of rice vinegar, and 2 tablespoons of Thai green curry paste. You can also add ½ teaspoon of dried chili flakes if you want some added heat. Stir the marinade just enough to blend the ingredients.

12. Empty the air fryer basket, then add the stir fry veggies. Lightly spray them with cooking spray, and cook them for 5 minutes.
13. In the largest bowl you have, combine: drained Shirataki noodles, dressing, tofu cubes, stir-fry vegetables, remaining sauce from stir-fry vegetables, and fresh vegetables. Toss the ingredients together with tongs, and top them with shrimp to serve.
14. If you divide the food into 6 servings, you will get 2 shrimp each.
15. Serve hot.

## Pasta Salad

This fresh pasta salad is combined with roasted vegetables to maximize flavor. It is a delicious salad that is low in calories and fat content. You will definitely love it!

*This recipe takes 40 minutes to prepare, 1 hour 45 minutes to cook and makes 8 servings of 1 cup each.*

*Fat 1.3 grams*
*Calories 121*

*Ingredients:*
- 4 Tomatoes, medium and cut in eighths
- 3 Eggplants, small
- 3 Zucchini, medium sized
- 2 Bell Peppers, any color
- 4 Cups Large Pasta, uncooked in any shape
- 1 Cup Cherry Tomatoes, sliced
- ½ Cup Italian Dressing, fat-free
- 8 Tablespoons Parmesan, grated
- 2 Tablespoon Extra Virgin Olive Oil
- 2 Teaspoon Pink Himalayan Salt
- 1 Teaspoon Basil, dried
- High Quality Cooking Spray

*Instructions:*
1. Wash eggplant, pat it dry and then slice off and discard the stem. Do not peel the eggplant. Slice it into ½ inch thick rounds.
2. Toss the eggplant with 1 tablespoon of extra virgin olive oil, and put the rounds in the air fryer basket.
3. Cook eggplant for 40 minutes at 160C (350F). Once it is soft and has no raw taste remaining, set the eggplant aside.
4. Wash the zucchini, pat it dry and then slice off and discard the stem. Do not peel the zucchini. Slice the zucchini into ½ inch

rounds. Toss together with extra virgin olive oil, and put it in the air fryer basket.
5. Cook zucchini for about 25 minutes at 160C (350F). Once it is soft with no raw taste remaining, set the zucchini aside.
6. Wash the tomatoes and slice them into eighths. Arrange them in the air fryer basket and spray gently with high quality cooking spray.
7. Roast the tomatoes for 30 minutes at 160C (350F). Once they have shrunk and are starting to brown, set them aside.
8. Cook the pasta according to the directions on the package, drain them through a colander, and run them under cold water. Set them aside so they will cool off.
9. Wash the bell peppers, cut them in half, take off the stem and remove the seeds. Rinse under water if you need to, and then pat them dry.
10. Wash the cherry tomatoes and cut them in half.
11. In a large bowl, combine bell peppers and cherry tomatoes. Then, add in the roasted vegetables, cooked pasta, pink Himalayan salt, dressing, chopped basil leaves, and grated parmesan. Mix thoroughly.
12. Set the salad in the fridge to chill and marinade.
13. Serve the salad chilled or at room temperature.

# Simple Risotto

Risotto is a delicious rice based meal that can be enjoyed by itself or with anything added. In this cookbook, we have included a few risotto variations. This simple risotto recipe is the perfect opportunity for you to make your own variation or enjoy it simply as is.

*This recipe takes 15 minutes to prepare, 45 minutes to cook and makes 6 servings of 1/2 cup each.*

*Fat 2.9 grams*
*Calories 221*

Ingredients:
- 1 ½ Cups Risotto Rice
- 1.5 L Vegetable or Chicken Stock, heated
- 1 Tablespoon Extra Virgin Olive Oil

Instructions:
1. Put a tablespoon of extra virgin olive oil in the basket of your air fryer and let it warm for 2 minutes at 160C (320F).
2. Add the risotto rice and then cook for 3 minutes.
3. All at once, add your stock of choice. Cook the for 30 minutes.
4. If you are going to add any additional ingredients, now is the time.
5. Check to see how soft and creamy the rice is. If you need to, add some boiling water to the rice and cook it for an additional 5 minutes or so.
6. Serve hot.

## Sweet Potato and Mushroom Risotto

This hearty risotto is made with barley, mushroom and sweet potatoes. It is full of delicious seasoning, vegetables, and tastes delicious. You can enjoy this as a main dish, or paired with a meat such as chicken or steak.

*This recipe takes 15 minutes to prepare, 55 minutes to cook and makes 8 servings of 1 cup each.*

*Fat 3.5 grams*
*Calories 211*

*Ingredients:*
- 2 Onions, medium and chopped
- 2 Pounds Sweet Potato, peeled and diced
- 2 Garlic Cloves, crushed and minced
- ¾ Pound Pearl Barley
- 1 Can Mushrooms, sliced
- 5 Cups Stock, any flavor
- ¼ Cup Parmesan Cheese, grated
- 3 oz Skim Milk
- 3 Tablespoons Extra Virgin Olive Oil
- 1 Teaspoon Tarragon, dried
- 1 Teaspoon Thyme, dried

*Instructions:*
1. In a large stock pan, boil the stock.
2. In the air fryer basket, warm 2 tablespoons of extra virgin olive oil (save 1 tablespoon) at 160C (320F) for 1 minutes.
3. When the oil is warmed, add the diced sweet potatoes, and cook for 10 minutes.
4. After the 10 minutes is up, add the onion and minced garlic and cook for 5 minutes.
5. Add the pearl barley and cook for another 5 minutes.

6. After the 5 minutes is up, add 4 cups of the hot stock all at once (reserve 1 cup for later), and cook the mixture for 30 minutes.
7. Once the 30 minutes are over, adjust the liquidity of the mixture to your preferences with the additional stock, then add the can of mushrooms, milk, parmesan cheese, thyme, and tarragon.
8. Cook the mixture for another 5 to 7 minutes or so.
9. Serve immediately, piping hot.

## Turkey Mushroom Patties

These turkey mushroom patties are a delicious spin on burger patties that your family will definitely love. They are juicy, full of flavor, and are extremely healthy. You can alter the herbs to adjust to your taste, but the spices featured here make a scrumptious combination that will leave you wanting more.

*This recipe takes 10 minutes to prepare, 10 minutes to cook and makes 5 servings of 1 patty each.*

*Fat 6.1 grams*
*Calories 132*

*Ingredients:*
- 1 ¼ Pounds Ground Turkey, extra lean
- 6 White Mushrooms, medium and pureed in a food processor
- 1 Tablespoon Maggi sauce
- 1 Teaspoon Onion Powder
- 1 Teaspoon Garlic Powder
- Salt and Ground Black Pepper to Taste
- High Quality Cooking Spray

*Instructions:*
1. Thoroughly wash the mushrooms, shake them dry, and then put them in the food processor. Process until they are pureed into a paste.
2. Open the food processor and add: Maggi sauce, onion powder, garlic powder, salt and pepper to taste. Process until the ingredients are well blended.
3. In a large mixing bowl, add the ground turkey and then mix in the contents of your processor. Mix the two together with your hands, without over working the meat. If you blend the meat *too* much it will wind up with a tough and undesirable texture.
4. Divide the turkey and mushroom mixture into 5 even portions and form them into patties. Make an indentation in the center

with your thumb to prevent the patties from bunching up and encourage even cooking.
5. Spray the patties with high quality cooking spray lightly on both sides.
6. Preheat your air fryer to 160C (320F)
7. When it's hot, put the patties in the basket of your air fryer. Don't stack them: if you need to, cook in 2 batches. It is okay if the sides are touching, though.
8. Cook the patties for 10 minutes, or until they reach your desired doneness. You do not need to flip them at any point.
9. Serve hot over rice with gravy, in a bun like a regular burger, or however else you desire.

## Turkey Risotto

This turkey risotto is easy to make, full of flavor, and will definitely keep you full. It is a wonderful comfort food that is guilt-free. You can make it in a pinch, or make it ahead of time and reheat it later, such as with meal prepping. It can also be served as is, or alongside a delicious slice of baked turkey.

*This recipe takes 30 minutes to prepare, 1 hour to cook and makes 6 servings of 2 cups each.*

*Fat 13.7 grams*
*Calories 416*

*Ingredients:*
- 2 Onions, medium and chopped
- 2 Cans of Mushrooms, 8oz each and drained
- 5 Cups Stock, either vegetable or turkey
- 2 Cups Turkey, chopped
- 2 Cups Beer
- 1 ½ Cups Risotto Rice
- ½ Cup Parmesan Cheese, grated
- 3 Tablespoons Extra Virgin Olive Oil, divided into 2 tablespoons and 1 tablespoon
- 1 Tablespoon Butter
- 1 Teaspoon Basil, dried
- 1 Teaspoon Oregano, dried

*Instructions:*
1. In a large stock pot, boil the stock and then set it aside.
2. Wash, peel and then chop your onions.
3. Toss your onions with 2 tablespoons of extra virgin olive oil, and then heat them in your air fryer basket at 160C (320F) for 5 minutes.

4. Add the drained mushrooms, oregano and basil to the air fryer basket with the precooked onions. Cook the mixture for another 10 minutes.
5. In the warmed mixture, add the final tablespoon of extra virgin olive oil, as well as the risotto rice. Cook the mixture for 5 more minutes.
6. Add the beer, and then cook for another 5 minutes.
7. Then, add the turkey and hot stock, and cook for 25 minutes.
8. Finally, add the butter and grated parmesan cheese, and cook for a final 5 minutes.
9. This should be cooked al dente. You can add another 5-10 minutes if you prefer softer rice.
10. Serve immediately with a sprinkle of grated parmesan cheese and a drizzle of extra virgin olive oil.

# Chapter 4: Desserts

These sweet desserts are some of the best you might ever taste. They are satisfying, scrumptious, and taste exactly like a gourmet dessert. You and your family will be so impressed that dessert took little effort to prepare and tastes so amazing!

**10 Minute Chocolate Profiteroles**
These sweet profiteroles have a creamy filling and are topped with a delicious chocolate sauce. They are easy to make, take almost no time at all to prepare, and are a wonderful way to end any meal.

*This recipe takes 15 minutes to prepare, 20 minutes to cook and makes 9 servings of 1 piece each.*

*Fat 11.9 grams*
*Calories 182*

*Ingredients:*
- (*Profiteroles*)
- 1 Cup Flour, lightly packed
- 1 ¼ Cup Water
- ½ Cup Butter
- 6 Eggs, medium
- (*Cream Filling*)
- 1 ¼ Cup Whipped Cream
- 2 Teaspoons Vanilla Extract
- 2 Teaspoons Icing Sugar, lightly packed
- (*Chocolate Sauce*)
- 100g Milk Chocolate, either chips or baker's chocolate broken into chunks
- ¼ Cup Butter

- 2 Tablespoons Whipped Cream
- (*Other Ingredients*)
- High Quality Cooking Spray
- Extra Icing Sugar, for garnish

*Instructions:*
1. *For the Profiteroles:*
   a. Preheat your air fryer to 170C (340F)
   b. In a large pan, bring the water and butter to a boil. Combine them thoroughly.
   c. Remove the mixture from the heat, and slowly mix the flour in a bit at a time.
   d. Return the pan to the heat and gently combine until they form a large dough in the middle of the pan.
   e. Set the dough aside and let it cool down.
   f. Add the eggs to the dough and knead together until it is well combined and the mixture is smooth.
   g. Divide the dough into 9 portions, and turn each portion into a circular profiterole shape.
   h. Lightly spray the air fryer basket and then cook the profiteroles for 10 minutes at 180C (350F).
   i. NOTE: The cooking profiteroles should not touch each other or be layered. Cook in two batches if necessary.
2. *For the Cream Filling:*
   a. In a medium mixing bowl, whisk together the vanilla essence, whipped cream and icing sugar until it thickens into a creamy filling.
3. *For the Chocolate Sauce:*
   a. Make a double boiler by putting a glass bowl over a pot of boiling water, make sure there is a gap between the two for air to flow (you can do this with a metal fork or two), and don't let the water evaporate or touch the bottom of the glass bowl.) Or, use a double boiler you may have on hand.
   b. Melt together the chocolate, butter, and cream in the glass bowl. Mix it well until you have a melted chocolate mixture.
   c. Alternatively, you could microwave the ingredients in a glass bowl in 30-45 second intervals and mix thoroughly in between each interval.

4. *To Assemble:*
    a. Cut the profiteroles in half and fill the center with the cream filling.
    b. Cover the profiteroles with chocolate sauce and, if you desire, sprinkle the top with icing sugar.
    c. Serve warm.

# British Victoria Sponge Cake

This elegant sponge cake is a British delicacy that you can make and then bake right in your air fryer! This variation has a fruity strawberry and cream filling to compliment the fluffy white sponge cake. It tastes just like the tasty traditional classic and pairs lovely with a black tea for dessert, or low tea time. You will definitely fall in love with this recipe and its delicious flavor.

*This recipe takes 15 minutes to prepare, 28 minutes to cook and makes 8 servings of 1 piece each.*

*Fat 20.0 grams*
*Calories 297*

*Ingredients:*
- *(Victoria Sponge Cake)*
- ¾ Cup Plain Flour
- ¾ Cup Caster Sugar
- ½ Cup Butter
- 2 Eggs, medium and beaten
- *(Strawberry and Cream Filling)*
- ¾ Cup Icing Sugar, sifted
- ¼ Cup Butter
- 2 Tablespoon Strawberry Jam
- 1 Tablespoon Whipped Cream

*Instructions:*
1. *For the Victorian Sponge Cake*
    a. Start by preheating the air fryer to 180C (350F) for about 10 minutes.
    b. While the air fryer heats up, grease a baking dish that is small enough to fit in your air fryer, but big enough to make a decent sized cake.
    c. In a medium bowl, cream together the butter and sugar until they create a light and fluffy texture.

d. Take the beaten eggs and combine them into the butter and sugar mixture. Blend well.
   e. Once the ingredients are thoroughly mixed, add the flour a little at a time. Fold it in slowly until there is no remaining flour.
   f. Pour the mixture into your greased baking dish and bake for 15 minutes.
   g. After the 15 minutes, lower the temperature to 170C (338F) and bake for an additional 10 minutes.
   h. Remove the cake from the air fryer and let it cool until it is room temperature.
2. *The Strawberry and Cream Filling*
   a. In a medium mixing bowl, cream the butter until it is light and fluffy.
   b. Add the icing sugar slowly until it is all gone and then mix well.
   c. Finally, add the whipped cream and beat the ingredients together until they are thick and creamy.
3. *To Assemble:*
   a. Slice the cooled cake in half so you have two even layers of cake. Carefully place the top layer on a plate while you assemble the filling.
   b. On the bottom layer of cake, spread out an even coat of strawberry jam until the entire layer is covered with a healthy amount.
   c. Put the cream filling in a piping bag and pipe it over the strawberry jam layer until you have none left.
   d. Replace the top layer of the cake and very gently press them together.
4. Serve immediately or store in an air tight container in the fridge for up to 3 days.

## Chocolate Brownies and Homemade Caramel Sauce

These dreamy chocolate brownies are the fluffiest brownies that will definitely curb your craving for something chocolatey and sweet. They are topped with a drizzle of homemade caramel sauce, and will leave your taste buds dancing.

*This recipe takes 20 minutes to prepare, 18 minutes to cook and makes 4 servings of 1 piece each.*

*Fat 1.5 grams*
*Calories 130*

*Ingredients:*
- 2 Eggs, medium and beaten
- 1 ¼ Cup Brown Sugar
- 1 Cup Self-Rising Flour, lightly packed
- 2/3 Cup Caster Sugar
- ½ Cup Butter
- ¼ Cup Milk
- ¼ Cup Chocolate Chips
- 2 Tablespoons Water, room temperature
- 2 Teaspoons Vanilla Extract
- High Quality Cooking Spray

*Instructions:*
1. *For the Brownies:*
    a. Preheat your air fryer to 180C (350F) for about 10 minutes.
    b. While the air fryer heats up, start preparing your brownies by melting the butter and chocolate in a double boiler.
    c. Once the chocolate and butter are completely melted together, blend in the brown sugar.
    d. Next, add the eggs and then the vanilla extract. Mix thoroughly.

e. Finally, slowly add the self-rising flour. Blend the entire batter until all of the ingredients are completely combined.
   f. Lightly spray a cooking dish that will fit in your air fryer with high quality cooking spray, and then add the batter to your dish. Put the dish in the air fryer.
   g. Cook the brownies in the air fryer for 15 minutes at the preheated temperature.
2. *For the Caramel Sauce:*
   a. In a pan over medium heat, mix together the caster sugar and water until the sugar is completely melted.
   b. Turn up the heat a bit and cook the sugar for about 3 minutes, until it turns a light brown color.
   c. Remove the sugar from the heat and after 2 minutes, stir in the butter and keep blending until the two are completely combined and the butter is melted.
   d. Finally, stir in the milk slowly.
   e. Set the caramel sauce aside to cool.
3. *To Assemble:*
   a. Remove the brownie from the cooking pan and cut it into 4 squares.
   b. Place each square on a plate and drizzle your desired amount of caramel sauce over top of the brownies.
   c. If you'd like, you can add bananas, strawberries or any other fruit to the dish as a garnish.

## Chocolate Muffins

These sweet chocolate muffins make wonderful desserts, or can even be served up as a tasty snack! They are full of flavor and delicious sweetness that will leave your mouth watering. Plus, they are simple to make!

*This recipe takes 10 minutes to prepare, 15 minutes to cook and makes 12 servings of 1 piece each.*

*Fat 6.0 grams*
*Calories 210*

*Ingredients:*
- 2 1/8 Cups Caster Sugar
- 2 Cups Self-Rising Flour
- ½ Cup Butter
- 1/8 Cup Milk Chocolate, chips or broken up chunks of baker's chocolate
- 5 Tablespoons Milk
- 2 Tablespoons Cocoa Powder
- ½ Teaspoon Vanilla Extract
- 2 Eggs, medium
- Water

*Instructions:*
1. Start by preheating your air fryer to 180C (350F) for about 10 minutes.
2. In a large mixing bowl, combine the sugar and cocoa until it is completely mixed.
3. Cut in the butter by cutting it into small chunks and putting it in the sugar and cocoa mixture. Rub it in until the entire mixture has the consistency of breadcrumbs.
4. In a small mixing bowl, crack the eggs in and beat them together. Pour in the milk and then mix it into the eggs until they are thoroughly mixed.

5. Add the egg and milk mixture into the sugar mixture and blend the two together until they are completely combined.
6. Add the vanilla extract and mix the batter. If it is too thick, add some water, a little bit at a time, until it creates a cake batter consistency.
7. If you are using baker's chocolate or another large piece of chocolate, smash it under a rolling pin to create small chunks. If you are using chocolate chips, skip this step.
8. Mix the chocolate into the batter until it is evenly distributed.
9. Give the muffin batter a final mix to make sure everything is combined.
10. Spoon the batter into small, pre-greased bun cases until they are about 80% full.
11. Put the bun cases in the preheated air fryer and bake for 9 minutes.
12. Reduce the temperature to 160C (320F) and bake for an additional 6 minutes.
13. Serve hot with a side of vanilla ice cream or fresh fruit.
14. Alternatively, store in an air tight container in the fridge for up to 3 days.

## Double Chocolate Chip Cookies

This delicious double chocolate chip cookie dough recipe is an amazing cookie recipe. It is the perfect comfort food. This pan-style cookie will definitely have you drooling.

*This recipe takes 5 minutes to prepare, 20 minutes to cook and makes 9 servings of 1 piece each.*

*Fat 9.0 grams*
*Calories 210*

*Ingredients:*
- 1 ¼ Cup Self-Rising Flour
- 2/3 Cup Chocolate Chips, any kind or bakers chocolate
- 1/3 Cup Brown Sugar
- ½ Cup Butter
- 4 Tablespoons Honey
- 1 Tablespoon Milk
- High Quality Cooking Spray

*Instructions:*
1. Start by preheating your air fryer to 160C (320F) for about 10 minutes.
2. In the meantime, use a large mixing bowl to cream the butter until it is soft.
3. Add the sugar and cream together and blend until they are light and fluffy.
4. Once the mix has reached your desired texture, mix in the honey.
5. Slowly fold in the flour until it has all been added.
6. If you are using baker's chocolate, use a rolling pin to smash it up to give yourself chunks of all different sizes. If you are using chocolate chips, skip this step.
7. Add the chocolate to your cookie dough and blend well so they are evenly distributed throughout the dough.
8. Pour in the milk and thoroughly stir the mixture.

9. Lightly spray your air fryer basket with a high quality cooking spray. Dump or spoon the entire cookie dough mixture into it.
10. Cook the dough for 20 minutes.
11. Cut into 9 portions and serve immediately or store in an air tight container for up to 3 days.

# Mini Apple Pies

These modern apple pies taste just like the ones Grandma makes. You will love how delicious they are. Plus, they are incredibly simple and are baked right on your countertop, in your air fryer!

*This recipe takes 5 minutes to prepare, 18 minutes to cook and makes 9 servings of 1 piece each.*

*Fat 18.05 grams*
*Calories 360*

*Ingredients:*
- 2 Red Apples, medium. McIntosh are best
- Water
- ¾ Cup Flour, lightly packed
- 1/8 Cup Butter
- 1 Tablespoon Caster Sugar
- A Pinch of Caster Sugar
- A Pinch of Cinnamon

*Instructions:*
1. *To Make the Pastry:*
    a. Pour your flour in a medium mixing bowl. Cut in your butter by cutting it into small chunks and putting the chunks in the flour. Using the back of a fork, or a pastry blender, rub the butter into the flour until it is well blended.
    b. Add the sugar and mix it in thoroughly.
    c. Slowly add a tiny bit of water at a time while you are blending the ingredients together until you get a moist, smooth dough texture.
    d. Lightly coat your pastry tins with butter so your pastry doesn't stick.
    e. Roll out the pastry until it is about 1/8" thick, and cut it to fill your pastry tins.
2. *To Make the Filling:*

a. Wash, peel and then dice your apples into small chunks.
b. Evenly distribute the apples into your pie tins until there are none left.
c. Sprinkle the apples with sugar and cinnamon.
d. Using the left over pastry, make a top for your pies. Make some fork or knife slits into the pastry topping so that the pie can breathe and it cooks evenly.
e. Cook the pies for 18 minutes in your air fryer at the preheated temperature.

## Simple Shortbread Fingers

These buttery shortbread fingers are just like the ones you love to enjoy at tea time. They are creamy, crumbly, and taste so much better than store bought ones. Plus, they are healthier than other dessert options, too!

*This recipe takes 4 minutes to prepare, 12 minutes to cook and makes 10 servings of 1 piece each.*

*Fat 6.0 grams*
*Calories 100*

*Ingredients:*
- 1 ½ Cups Butter
- 1 Cup Plain Flour
- ¾ Cup Caster Sugar
- High Quality Cooking Spray

*Instructions:*
1. Start by preheating your air fryer to 180C (350F).
2. In a medium bowl, combine the flour and sugar.
3. Cut the butter into the mix by cutting it into small chunks and putting the chunks in the flour and sugar mixture. Using the back of a fork, rub the butter into the mixture until it is well combined.
4. Using your hands, knead the mixture until it is smooth and evenly combined.
5. Make the shortbread dough into 10 evenly sized finger shapes. If you desire, you can decorate them with fork markings.
6. Lightly spray the air fryer basket with high quality cooking spray and carefully line each of the 10 cookies in so that they are not touching each other.
7. Bake the shortbread cookies for 12 minutes.
8. Allow to cool slightly and then serve, or store in an air tight container and eat within' 3 days.

## Strawberry Cupcakes with Strawberry Frosting

These sweet strawberry cupcakes are so delicious you won't believe how easy they are. Plus, they are topped with your very own homemade strawberry frosting, too! They are so scrumptious you will want them for dessert every single night.

*This recipe takes 15 minutes to prepare, 8 minutes to cook and makes 10 servings of 1 piece each.*

*Fat 4.2 grams*
*Calories 150*

*Ingredients:*
- *(Cupcakes)*
- 1 Cup Self-Rising Flour
- ½ Cup Butter
- ½ Cup Caster Sugar
- 2 Medium Eggs
- ½ Teaspoon Vanilla Extract
- *(Icing)*
- 1 Cup Icing Sugar
- ¼ Cup Butter
- ¼ Cup Fresh Strawberries, blended or processed
- 1 Tablespoon Whipped Cream
- ½ Teaspoon Pink Food Coloring (optional)

*Instructions:*
1. *For the Cupcakes*
    a. Preheat the air fryer to 170C (340F).
    b. In a large mixing bowl, thoroughly blend the butter and sugar together. Continue folding together until the mixture becomes light and fluffy.
    c. Once the mixture reaches a desirable texture, blend in the vanilla extract and then the eggs one by one.

- d. Finally, mix in the flour a little at a time until it is completely mixed in. Fold the batter together until it reaches a desirable cake batter texture.
  - e. Put the batter into little bun cases until the cases are 80% full, and place them in the air fryer basket.
  - f. Bake them for 8 minutes at 170C (340F)
2. *For the Icing:*
  - a. In a medium mixing bowl, whip the butter until it is creamed.
  - b. Then, gradually add the icing sugar until the mixture is creamy and light.
  - c. If you are using food coloring, add it now.
  - d. Add the whipped cream and strawberry puree and then combine well until all of the ingredients are thoroughly blended.
3. *To Assemble:*
  - a. Remove the baked cupcakes from the air fryer and let them cool to about room temperature.
  - b. Put the icing in a piping bag and top the cupcakes in a circular motion.
  - c. Serve immediately or store in an air tight container in the fridge for up to 3 days.

# Chapter 5: Snacks

These tasty snacks are excellent to enjoy throughout the day when you're feeling a little hungry. They can be made ahead of time and packed in lunches, stored in the fridge for midnight cravings, or made when you are ready to enjoy them. Each snack is healthy, delicious, and so easy to make!

**Blooming Onion Flower**
This crispy blooming onion flower is beautiful to look at and makes a great variation for chips. It has the tasty cooked onion flavor with the crispiness of potato chips. It is best served with mayo or any other creamy dipping sauce.

*This recipe takes 2 hours 10 minutes to prepare, 20 minutes to cook and makes 4 servings of 1/4 of an onion each.*

*Fat 33.5 grams*
*Calories 488*

*Ingredients:*
- 1 White Onion, large
- 2 Eggs, large
- ¾ Cup Panko Breadcrumbs, or any other breadcrumbs you have on hand
- ¼ Cup Milk, fat-free
- 1 ½ Teaspoon Paprika
- 1 Teaspoon Garlic Powder
- 1 Teaspoon Pink Himalayan Salt
- ½ Teaspoon Cajun Seasoning
- ½ Teaspoon Ground Black Pepper

*Instructions:*
1. In a medium bowl, combine bread crumbs, olive oil and Cajun seasoning until it is thoroughly blended.
2. In another mixing bowl, combine the salt and pepper.
3. In a third bowl, blend together the milk and egg.
4. Peel the onion and cut into a bloom: starting a ½ inch from the root, cut downward all the way into the cutting board. Repeat until you have 4 cuts around the onion that are evenly spaced. Continue by slicing evenly between each of the 4 cuts until you have 8 total cuts.
5. Fill ice water into a bowl large enough to entirely submerge the onion. Let it soak for at least 2 hours, or as long as overnight.
6. When it is done soaking, remove the onion from water and pat dry.
7. Open the onion to expose the inner layers, creating the flowers' "petals"
8. In a medium bowl, combine bread crumbs, olive oil and Cajun seasoning until it is thoroughly blended.
9. In another mixing bowl, combine the salt and pepper.
10. In a third bowl, blend together the milk and egg.
11. Place the onion in a bowl and sprinkle it with the salt and pepper mixture.
12. Ladle the egg mixture generously into every single crevice of the onion. When done, turn the onion upside down to drain excess egg off and then place it on a fresh dish.
13. Cover the onion with the breadcrumb mixture, pressing it in so it stays in place. Make sure you cover every surface entirely.
14. Preheat the air fryer to 182C (360F) for about 10 minutes.
15. When the air fryer is hot, put the onion in and then cover it with a makeshift tent made of aluminum foil.
16. Cook it for 10 minutes. Leave the foil on while it cooks.
17. After 10 minutes, check the crispness of the onion. Replace the foil and add another 5-10 minutes to cook the onion to your desired crispness.
18. When the onion is done, remove it from the air fryer and serve it with your choice of dipping sauce.
19. You can either serve the onion whole and share it between four people, or cut it into 4 even portions and serve it individually. Serving it individually will ruin the flower appearance, however.

# Feta Triangles

These crispy feta triangles are full of delicious flavor. They are tasty, go great with a dipping sauce or on their own, and are somewhat addicting! Their cheesy flavor is paired with wonderful seasoning to make these the ultimate snack food.

*This recipe takes 20 minutes to prepare, 10 minutes to cook and makes 5 servings of 3 pieces each.*

*Fat 7.0 grams*
*Calories 90*

Ingredients:
- 5 Sheets Filo Pastry, defrosted
- 1 Scallion, finely chopped
- 4oz Feta Cheese
- 1 Egg, medium and yolk only
- 2 Tablespoons Parsley, flat-leafed and finely chopped
- 2 Tablespoons Extra Virgin Olive Oil
- Pink Himalayan Salt and Ground Black Pepper, to taste

Instructions:
1. In a medium bowl, beat the egg yolk until it is smooth.
2. Add the feta cheese, chopped parsley and chopped scallion to the yolk and blend until the ingredients are well combined.
3. Dust the mixture with pink Himalayan salt and ground black pepper, to taste.
4. Prepare the filo pastries on a flat surface and cut them into 3 strips each, totaling 15 strips.
5. For each strip of pastry, take a full scoop of the seasoned mixture and pour it on the underside of the pastry strip, forming a triangle. Fold the strip in a zig zag way until the filling is completely wrapped in a triangular shape.
6. Repeat the above process until every single filo strip has been used and there is no seasoned mixture left.
7. Preheat your air fryer to 198C (390F) for about 10 minutes.

8. Gently brush each stuffed filo pastry with some extra virgin olive oil and place enough triangles in the hot air fryer basket to fill it without over lapping each other. (It should fit about 5 triangles, meaning you will need to cook 5 batches.)
9. Put the basket in the air fryer and cook the pastries for about 3 minutes, or until the pastries have a golden brown color.
10. Repeat the cooking process for the remaining batches.
11. Serve the triangles hot, or store them in an air tight container for up to 3 days.

## Rosemary Yam Potato Chips

These delicious, crunchy chips are flavorful and healthy. They are a wonderful spin on traditional potato chips, but have the same great texture and flavor.

*This recipe takes 40 minutes to prepare, 30 minutes to cook and makes 2 servings of 1 cup each.*

*Fat 7.0 grams*
*Calories 139*

*Ingredients:*
- 2 Yam Potatoes, medium to large
- 1 Tablespoon Extra Virgin Olive Oil
- 1 Teaspoon Rosemary, fresh and chopped or dried and flaked
- A Pinch of Pink Himalayan Salt
- Water

*Instructions:*
1. Thoroughly clean the yam potatoes and then thinly slice them to make the potato chips. You can use a mandolin at this point to get an even, thin cut for the chips.
2. Fill a large bowl or pot with water and put the chips into the water.
3. Let the potato slices soak for 30 minutes, giving them a good mix with your hands and changing the water every 5 minutes. This eliminates a good deal of the starch, makes them crispier and helps them keep their color.
4. Completely drain the water from the bowl and pat the potato slices dry with a paper towel. They need to be completely dried.
5. Heat your air fryer to 165C (330F) for about 5-10 minutes or until warmed.
6. In a clean mixing bowl, toss the potato slices together with extra virgin olive oil until they are evenly coated.

7. Place the potato slices into the air fryer basket and cook for 30 minutes, or until golden brown.
8. While cooking, shake the basket every 5 minutes or so to make sure they cook evenly and don't stick together in a large clump.
9. When the chips are done, dump them into a large, clean bowl.
10. Sprinkle fresh (or dried) rosemary over the chips, as well as a light dusting of pink Himalayan salt. Toss the chips to distribute the seasoning evenly through the chips.
11. Serve warm or store in an air tight container at room temperature for 3 days.

# Simple Gourmet Potato Chips

What would a fried food cook book be without a potato chip recipe? These gourmet potato chips are better than anything you'll buy in store, plus they're inexpensive and take almost no effort to prepare. We have chosen to flavor them with the healthy pink Himalayan salt, but you can use anything you desire on your own. Mix it up and play with the flavors to find what you really love!

*This recipe takes 10 minutes to prepare, 50 minutes to cook and makes 4 ½ servings of ¾ cup each.*

*Fat 3.5 grams*
*Calories 201*

*Ingredients:*
- 2 Pounds Potatoes (2 large Russets)
- 1 Tablespoon Duck Fat (or coconut oil)
- Pink Himalayan Salt, to taste

*Instructions:*
1. Thoroughly wash the potatoes and then peel them.
2. Slice the potatoes thinly, you can use a mandolin if you have one to simplify this step
3. Fill a large bowl with cold water and let the potato slices soak for about 30 minutes. You can swish them around a bit if you want. (This helps eliminate the starch, prevent discoloration, and make an overall crispier chip)
4. Heat the air fryer for 160C (320F) and melt the duck fat (or coconut oil) for 2 minutes.
5. Thoroughly drain the potato slices and pat them completely dry.
6. Add the potato slices to the air fryer basket and cook for 40 or 50 minutes, checking on them every 10 minutes. Each time

you check on them, use a pair of tongs to break up the clumps and spread them back out so they cook evenly.
7. Transfer the crisps to a bowl, and toss them with a few dashes of sea salt until they are your desired flavor.
8. Serve chips hot or warm for best flavor, or store in an air tight container and eat them later.

# Conclusion

Thank you for purchasing and reading *Air Fryer Cookbook: Easy to Make Air Fryer Recipes for Every Taste*. This simple cookbook is a wonderful starting point for anyone who is learning to use their air fryer as a staple in their home cooking. Each recipe was carefully selected to help introduce you to the wonderful world of air fryer frying, cooking, baking, grilling, and more!

I hope that this book has provided you with some favorite recipes to help you master the art of using your air fryer. I also hope that you learned how much you can do with the air fryer, and have realized that the sky is the limit!

The next step is to test out a few, or a bunch, of your favorite recipes from this book. You can enjoy them yourself as a part of meal prepping, or share them with family and friends! None of you will believe that these delicious recipes came from an air fryer appliance that sits on your counter top!

Finally, if you enjoyed this cookbook and felt it added value to your air frying experience, I ask that you please take the time to review it on Amazon. Your honest opinion would be greatly appreciated!

Thank you, and best of luck in your air frying adventures!

# Air Fryer Cookbook

## More Fancier Air Fryer Recipes For Every Taste!

© **Copyright 2016 Simon Donovan - All rights reserved.**

This document is geared towards providing exact and reliable information in regards to the topic and issue covered. The publication is sold with the idea that the publisher is not required to render accounting, officially permitted, or otherwise, qualified services. If advice is necessary, legal or professional, a practiced individual in the profession should be ordered.

- From a Declaration of Principles which was accepted and approved equally by a Committee of the American Bar Association and a Committee of Publishers and Associations.

In no way is it legal to reproduce, duplicate, or transmit any part of this document in either electronic means or in printed format. Recording of this publication is strictly prohibited and any storage of this document is not allowed unless with written permission from the publisher. All rights reserved.

The information provided herein is stated to be truthful and consistent, in that any liability, in terms of inattention or otherwise, by any usage or abuse of any policies, processes, or directions contained within is the solitary and utter responsibility of the recipient reader. Under no circumstances will any legal responsibility or blame be held against the publisher for any reparation, damages, or monetary loss due to the information herein, either directly or indirectly.

Respective authors own all copyrights not held by the publisher.

The information herein is offered for informational purposes solely, and is universal as so. The presentation of the information is without contract or any type of guarantee assurance.

The trademarks that are used are without any consent, and the publication of the trademark is without permission or backing by the trademark owner. All trademarks and brands within this book are for clarifying purposes only and are the owned by the owners themselves, not affiliated with this document.

# Table of Contents

Introduction ............................................................................ 1

Chapter 1: APPETIZERS ................................................................ 3

Chapter 2: ENTREES ............................................................... 12

Chapter 3: DESERTS ................................................................ 57

Conclusion .......................................................................... 80

# Introduction

Air fryer is definitely the new *hot* item in the kitchen appliance industry. In opposition to its oil-drenched counterpart, the air fryer cooks by circulating hot air around your food, giving it an overall cleaner and healthier taste than traditional oil frying.

The air fryer works by utilizing a non-digital, mechanical fan which allows for hot air circulation to flow around the food at high speeds. This allows the food to cook and produce a crispy layer thanks to a scientific discovery called the Maillard effect.

According to original french publication which discovered the Maillard effect, it is a "chemical reaction between amino acids and reducing sugars that gives browned food its desirable flavor. Seared steaks, pan-fried dumplings, cookies and other kinds of biscuits, breads, toasted marshmallows, and many other foods undergo this reaction. It is named after French chemist Louis-Camille Maillard, who first described it in 1912 while attempting to reproduce biological protein synthesis".

By circulating hot air that reaches up to temperatures of 392 degrees, the air fryer fries many different types of foods and uses a much smaller amount of oil than regular fryers. There are a lot of air fryers that are currently in the market that are fitted with adjustable temperature handles (as well as timers). These adjustable temperature handles make your cooking experience much more accurate with more precise temperatures.

Many air fryer brands use 80% less cooking oil compared to many traditional fryers. According to one of the more well-known air fryer brands out there, "while most models of air fryers require that the basket is periodically shaken to ensure even cooking throughout, some models incorporate a food agitator that continuously churns the food during the cooking process. By using less oil to fry, air fryers become a healthier alternative to traditionally deep fried foods which can increase the risk of cardiovascular diseases, hypertension, diabetes, cancer and obesity".

One of the great benefits to the air fryer is that in today's fast-paced world, more people are now choosing much healthier options for eating and the air fryer's ability to use less oil to cook great food contributes to a healthier, cleaner diet. For those of us who really enjoy fried food, it's hard to simply curb those cravings and food traditions. This is why opting for the air fryer is a tastier, healthier, and economically friendly option for frying food.

Air Fryers are incredibly easy to use and the basket that it is packaged with fits perfectly into the pan it comes with (both of which are easily able to fit into the air fryers many cooking compartments). The hot-air circulation and the timer will make your cooking experience with the air fryer easy and accessible from the most pro-chef to the most novice home cooks. After deciding what it is you want to make, just put your ingredients into the air fryer and set the timer. It will take some time but then the hot air will begin to circulate and you will hear a ding sound indicating that the meal is ready.

Don't know what you want to cook? Well luckily, this book has over 70 great, fancy, and delectable recipes for you to try out. With simple instructions that will come with your air fryer and this recipe guide, you should be able to have a great time cooking with the air fryer. The number one way to go about figuring out the best things to cook with your air fryer is to think about everyday meals that you make with other appliances.

The air fryer can help you get rid of your oven, deep fryer, and stove top. Air fryers are mainly used for frying, baking, grilling, roasting. The air fryer is able to fry because of the various parts it's made up of, bake, grill, and roast; all in one handy appliance.

Ultimately, the various foods are available in this guide, ranging from deserts to the most exotic dinner fare, so there's much to choose from.

# Chapter 1: APPETIZERS

## Macaroni and Fontina Gateau

Serving Size: 2
Preparation Time: 14 minutes
Nutritional Information: 200 calories per serving

INGREDIENTS

½ cup milk (whole)
¼ cup crumbs of bread
½ cup gruyere or mozzarella cheese
½ teaspoon paprika
1 tablespoon unsalted butter, melted
¼ teaspoon ground black pepper
¼ cup parmesan cheese
½ cup heavy cream
⅛ teaspoon ground nutmeg
½ cup grated Fontina cheese
½ cup grated sharp cheddar cheese
salt to taste
½ pound pasta (elbow)

INSTRUCTIONS

Place cooked pasta into a deep, round, casserole pan. You can begin to create a rue in a separate bowl using the bread crumbs, Parmesan cheese and butter. Stir this mixture to blend. Add milk, heavy cream, Fontina, Gruyere, Cheddar, Essence, the remaining 1/2 teaspoon of salt, black pepper and nutmeg and stir well to combine.

Place pan in the basket of the Air Fryer, and close the drawer. Set the temperature to 350 degrees Fahrenheit for 30 minutes. After 30 minutes, take the pan out from inside of the fryer and allow the gateau to cool for at least 20 minutes before inverting the deep casserole pan over a plate and removing the pan to release the mac & cheese.

Cut into wedges and serve warm.

## Fancy Tortilla Chips

Serving Size: 2
Preparation Time: 1 minute
Nutritional Information: 160 calories per serving

INGREDIENTS

8 corn tortillas
Salt to taste
1 tbsp olive oil

INSTRUCTIONS

Set temperature to 200 degrees Fahrenheit. Cut corn tortillas into triangles. Brush with olive oil. Place tortilla pieces in wire basket in small batches and air fry for 3 minutes. Repeat until all tortilla chips are cooked. Sprinkle with salt. Serve.

## Vegetable Spring Rolls Recipe

Serving Size: 2
Preparation Time: 1 minute
Nutritional Information: 160 calories per serving

INGREDIENTS

Roll:
10 Spring roll sheets
2 tbsp corn flour (you can substitute for maida if necessary)
Water

Stuffing:
2 cups shredded cabbage
1 carrot
2 whole onions
½ teaspoon capsicum
1 whole ginger
1 whole garlic clove
Pinch of sugar
1 tbsp pepper powder
1 teaspoon soy sauce
Salt to taste
2 tbsp cooking oil
2 spring onions (for garnish)

INSTRUCTIONS

Defrost spring rolls until soft and room temperature. Chop carrots, onions, ginger, garlic, and capsicum into thin slices. Chopping everything quickly will ensure quick cooking
Set air fryer temperature to 180 degrees. Roll filling into the spring roll. Use a brush to lightly add oil to the spring rolls. Place rolls in air fryer basket.

Bake the rolls in the air fryer for 10 minutes. Remove the basket from the air fryer and flip each spring roll over to ensure that it is properly baked on both sides of the spring roll. If rolls remain white, bake it for another 2-3 minutes. Remove and serve hot.

## Gluten-Free Salmon Croquettes

Serving Size: 4
Preparation Time: 10 minute
Nutritional Information: 120 calories per serving

INGREDIENTS

2 eggs (beaten, lightly)
1 large tin of red salmon (drained)
1 cup bread crumbs
⅓ cup vegetable oil
½ bunch of parsley, roughly chopped
⅛ teaspoon black pepper

INSTRUCTIONS

Preheat air fryer to 200 degrees. Mix together the salmon and mix with herbs, egg, and the seasoning.

Mix together the bread crumbs and oil in another bowl, until you get a loose mixture that can act as a glue for our croquettes. Shape the salmon mix into 16 small croquettes, and coat them in the crumb mixture.

In batches, put the croquettes in the basket and slide into the Air Fryer. Wait until golden brown.

Serve.

## Sage & Onion Stuffing Balls

Serving Size: 6
Preparation Time: 20 minute
Nutritional Information: 400 calories per serving

INGREDIENTS
2 lbs. sausage meat
½ Onion
½ tsp garlic puree
1 tsp sage
3 tbsp breadcrumbs
Pinch of salt
Black pepper

INSTRUCTIONS
Place all of your ingredients into a large bowl for mixing and make sure your ingredients are mixed well. Form into medium sized balls and place them in the Air Fryer. Cook at 180 degrees for 15 minutes. Serve and enjoy!

# Coconut Shrimp

Serving Size: 16-20
Preparation Time: 12 minutes
Nutritional Information: 120 calories per shrimp

INGREDIENTS

½ tsp salt
1 lb large shrimp (about 16 to 20 peeled/de-veined)
½ cup flour
2 egg whites
½ cup fine breadcrumbs
½ cup shredded unsweetened coconut zest of one lime
¼ teaspoon cayenne pepper
spray can of vegetable or canola oil
sweet chili sauce or duck sauce (for serving)

INSTRUCTIONS

Whisk the eggs in a shallow dish. Combine the breadcrumbs, coconut, lime zest, salt and cayenne pepper in another dish.

Pre-heat the air fryer to 400 degrees.

Dip each shrimp into the flour. Next, dip the shrimp into the egg mixture, and then into the breadcrumb coconut mixture to coat all sides. Place the breaded shrimp on a plate and spray with oil. Air fry shrimp but don't overcrowd basket. Cook the shrimp for five to six minutes or before it gets to the point that each shrimp is firm and cooked.

Serve and make sure to enjoy.

## Buffalo Wings

Serving Size: 8
Preparation Time: 5 hours
Nutritional Information: 300 calories per wing

INGREDIENTS

Buffalo Sauce:
¼ cup hot sauce
3 tablespoons butter, melted

2 pounds chicken wings
3 tablespoons butter, melted
¼ cup hot sauce
salt, to taste

INSTRUCTIONS

Cut off and discard the wing tips. Divide the drumlets from the winglets. Place them in a large food holding device. Mix the melted butter and the hot sauce and stir to make sure it's blend well. Pour this mixture over the chicken wings and let the wings marinate for 4 hours to overnight.

Pre-heat the air-fryer to 400 degrees. Air fry the wings for 12 minutes. Take out of air fry and place onto a place, put extra sauce on the wings and mix. Toss them all back into the air fry basket for another 2 minutes to heat through and finish cooking.

While the wings are air-frying, combine the remaining 3 tablespoons of butter and ¼ cup of hot sauce.
Remove the wings from the air-fryer and toss them again in this sauce. Serve.

## Toasted Pumpkin Seeds

Serving Size: 4
Preparation Time: 30 minutes
Nutritional Information: 40 calories per seed

INGREDIENTS

1½ teaspoons salt
1 teaspoon smoked paprika
1½ cups pumpkin seeds
1 tbsp olive oil

INSTRUCTIONS

Bring two quarts of well-salted water and make sure they boil. Add the pumpkin seeds to the boiling water and boil for 10 minutes. Drain the seeds and spread them out on paper towels to dry for at least 20 minutes.

Pre-heat the air-fryer to three-hundred and fifty degrees.

Mix the seeds with salt, olive oil, and smoked paprika and transfer them to the air-fryer basket. Air fry for 35 minutes.

Pumpkin seeds should be crispy and slightly browned. Allow the seeds to cool. Serve.

## Fried Pickles

Serving Size: 4
Preparation Time: 8 minutes
Nutritional Information: 100 calories per pickle

INGREDIENTS

½ tsp salt
½ tsp paprika
½ cup flour
1 jar of dill pickle wedges
1 egg
¼ cup milk
½ tsp garlic powder

INSTRUCTIONS

Whisk together milk and egg in one bowl. In another food holding device, combine all of your dry ingredients.

Dip the pickle wedges in flour mix, then egg mix, then back in flour mix. Heat 2 pickles in your oil for four to five minutes or before the pickles get cooked and become lightly brown.

Mindfully place the pickles into the oil and let cook for 2 to 3 minutes until it is golden brown. Place pickles on a plate and get ready to have your friends family grabbing for these delicious treats! Enjoy.

# Chapter 2: ENTREES

## Honey roasted carrots

Serving Size: 2
Preparation Time: 12 minutes
Nutritional Information: 30 calories

INGREDIENTS

1 tbsp Olive oil
Salt and pepper
3 cups of baby carrots or carrots cut into large chunks
1 tbsp Honey

INSTRUCTIONS

In a bowl, mix your carrots with your honey and the olive oil. Ensure carrots are well covered.
Season with salt and pepper. Cook in air fryer set to 200 degrees for 12 minutes. Serve while hot.

## Baked Garlic Parsley Potatoes

Serving Size: 3
Preparation Time: 1 hour
Nutritional Information: 300 calories

INGREDIENTS

1 tbsp salt

1 tsp parsley

3 potatoes

1 tbsp garlic

1 tbsp olive oil

INSTRUCTIONS
Using a fork, poke air holes into the potatoes. Sprinkle potatoes with the olive oil & seasonings. Using your hands, rub the potato seasoning evenly over each potato. As soon as you have the potatoes coated, you will want to put them into the air fryer basket and place them into the air fryer machine. Cook the potatoes on three-hundred and ninety two degrees for thirty-five to fourty minutes or until fork tender. You can use a variety of condiments to add a great taste to your potatoes, such as sour cream or even the more traditional staple-- parsley!

# Buttery Dinner Rolls

Serving Size: 4
Preparation Time: 2 hours
Nutritional Information: 30 calories

INGREDIENTS

1 milk (room temp)
Butter (softened)
1 ½ tsp salt
Sugar
2 Eggs
2¼ tsp instant yeast
2 cups bread flour

Glaze:
Some melted butter

INSTRUCTIONS

In bread maker pan, put all the ingredients in order suggested by manufacturer, or in the order listed here. Select the dough setting on your air fryer. When the cycle has come to a complete stop, put dough on top of a surface that has been floured very lightly and begin to punch and knead the air out of the dough, to ensure rising when baking.

Divide dough into 22 portions and form into balls which are round. Put them in the air fryer basket that has been lined with baking sheet and slightly oiled on the edges of the basket. Cover with a slightly dampened cloth.

Preheat the air fryer to 160 degrees. Air Bake these buns at 160 degrees for ten to thirteen minutes, or until golden brown. As for the second batch, I've changed the temperature to 150 degrees with the same baking time - buns have lighter colors compare to the first batch. Brush some melted butter on the buns once it is done baking.

# Old Fashioned Onion Rings

Serving Size: 2
Preparation Time: 12 minutes
Nutritional Information: 30 calories

INGREDIENTS

¾ cup bread crumbs
1 egg
1 tsp baking powder
1 very big onion (cut into ¼ inch slices)
1 cup milk
1 tsp salt
1 ¼ cups all purpose flour

INSTRUCTIONS

Separate all of the onion slices into rings to begin the structure for your delicious onion rings. In a separate bowl, stir and mix together all of your dry ingredients, including the salt, baking powder, and flour. Using a wide plate, spread bread crumbs around and now dredge the rings into the crumbs.

Make sure each onion ring is completely covered with the bread crumbs. Put the remainder of your onion rings into the air fryer and cook everything for seven to ten minutes at 360 degrees. You can open one of the onion rings to make sure it has cooked all the way through. Enjoy and serve!

## Avocado Fries

Serving Size: 3-4
Preparation Time: 12 minutes
Nutritional Information: 40 calories

INGREDIENTS

½ cup panko
½ teaspoon salt
1 Whole avocado
1 Ounce aquafaba

INSTRUCTIONS

Toss together the panko and salt in a shallow bowl. Pour the aquafaba into another shallow bowl.
Dredge the avocado slices in the aquafaba and then in the panko. Arrange the slices in a single layer in your air fryer basket. The single layer is important.

Air fry for 10 minutes at 390 degrees. Serve.

## Air-Fried Curly Fries

Serving Size: 4
Preparation Time: 12 minutes
Nutritional Information: 100 calories

INGREDIENTS

4 Russet Potatoes
Salt

INSTRUCTIONS

Run the potatoes through the large grates of a spiralizer, using kitchen shears to cut the curls after every 3 or 4 rotations. Put your potatoes into a bowl, add some water to the bowl, and let everything soak for about thirty minutes.

Preheat your air-fryer to three-hundred and sixty degrees. Drain the potatoes and rinse well. Put on a lined baking sheet and pat dry, removing as much moisture as possible. Now remove from the sheet and put contents into a bowl and add the canola oil. Season with salt and pepper and mix, making sure everything is coated. Place half of the potatoes in the fry basket and insert into the air fryer. Cook for 5 minutes, then increase the temperature to 390 degrees.

Pull out the basket and, using tongs, toss and stir the potatoes. Return the basket to the fryer. Continue cooking until the potatoes are cooked completely and golden brown on the outside, 10 to 12 minutes total, opening the basket 3 or 4 times during cooking to toss and stir them. Return the fryer temperature to 360 degrees and repeat to cook the remaining potatoes. Serve.

## Parmesan Sweet Potato Fries Recipe

Serving Size: 4
Preparation Time: 12 minutes
Nutritional Information: 250 calories

INGREDIENTS

2 lbs sweet potatoes
3 tablespoons grated parmesan cheese
Chopped parsley leaves (to garnish)
1 tablespoon olive oil
Pinch of salt

INSTRUCTIONS

Peel your potatoes and then rinse the sweet potatoes and cut into lengthwise strips. Soak the potatoes in a bowl of water for thirty minutes. Drain the water from the bowl and pat dry with paper towels. Place the sweet potatoes in a big bowl and add the salt and olive oil to the sweet potatoes and set aside.

Preheat the air fryer to three-hundred and thirty. Now place the potatoes in the air fryer cooking basket and allow the potatoes to cook for 5 minutes or until crisp and golden brown. Remove from the basket and allow to cool on countertop or stove top. Increase the temperature to 395 degrees and add the sweet potatoes back into the basket and cook for 10-15 minutes.

Transfer the sweet potato fries out of the air fryer and sprinkle the Parmesan cheese over the fries, mix gently and garnish with the parsley. Serve immediately.

## Fancy Homemade Mashed Potato Tater Tots

Serving Size: 4
Preparation Time: 12 minutes
Nutritional Information: 250 calories

INGREDIENTS

1 red potato

Salt and pepper

1 tsp oil
Parsley (to garnish)
1 teaspoon minced onion

INSTRUCTIONS

Chop potatoes and put them into a pot. Now add some water to make sure the pot of potatoes comes to a boil. Allow the potatoes to cook until al dente and then move them from the water and place in a bowl to dry. In a separate bowl combine the potatoes with the oil, onion, pepper, and salt. Preheat the air fryer to 379 degrees.

Begin to form tater tot shapes with the mashed potato mix and allow to bake for about seven to eight minutes. Toss the tots, then bake the potatoes for five minutes.

## Fried Zucchini Wedges

Serving Size: 8
Preparation Time: 12 minutes
Nutritional Information: 76 calories

INGREDIENTS

½ cup panko crumbs
¼ cup grated parmesan
¼ teaspoon basil
¼ teaspoon oregano
¼ teaspoon cayenne pepper
¼ cup egg white (about 2 egg whites)
2 medium-sized zucchini

INSTRUCTIONS

Mix together, in a bowl, cheese and herbs, the panko crumb. Set everything aside. Wash the zucchini well; leave unpeeled. Cut in half cross-wise, then cut into wedges not more than 1 cm thick. Put an egg white in a shallow bowl or place. Put a small amount of the crumb mixture on another plate.

Put zucchini wedge in the egg white to coat, then in the crumbs to coat, pressing down well. Then put in Air fryer basket. Repeat till all wedges are coated.

Take wedges out and put on a plate to cool. Serve.

## Baked Rice

Serving Size: 4
Preparation Time: 20 minutes
Nutritional Information: 400 calories

INGREDIENTS

2 tbsp of carrot cubes
1 veal sausage
8-10 tbsp of creamy sauce
1 tbsp butter
4 pieces of whole mince garlic
3 tbsp of broccoli (florets)
3 tbsp of shredded cheddar cheese
2 tbsp of shredded mozzarella cheese
2 packs overnight cooked rice

INSTRUCTIONS

Preheat air fryer for 5 minutes at temperature 180 degrees. Melt butter inside baking pan for about 2 minutes. Saute minced garlic for about one to two minutes or until fragrant. Add in broccoli florets and carrot cubes to fry for 4 minutes. Add a little water will help to speed up the softening. Add sausage slices and cook for 3 minutes or until they turn slightly browned. Add in the rice and mix well. Pour in the enough creamy sauce and mix well, level the rice with a ladle. Sprinkle cheese evenly and air fry for 8-10 minutes.

# Korean Sweet and Spicy Chicken Wings

Serving Size: 3
Preparation Time: 45 minutes
Nutritional Information: 200 calories

INGREDIENTS

¼ cup flour
¼ cup potato starch
1 tsp salt
Ten chicken wings
1 egg
1 tbsp frying oil
½ cup water or beer
½ cup dark brown sugar
⅓ cup roasted peanuts (chopped)
½ tsp ground red chili pepper
Three inch piece of fresh ginger
2 tbsp toasted sesame seeds
3 tbsp rice vinegar
½ cup light corn syrup or rice syrup
1 tsp red chili flakes
1 ½ tbsp soy sauce

INSTRUCTIONS

In a large bowl, mix together the starch, flour, 1/2 teaspoon ground chili pepper, egg, and salt until it's a thick (non-viscous) paste. Now add wings to the mixture and continue to mix until all the wings have the coating on them. Air fry the wings and sprinkle with your frying oil. Close your lid and allow to cook for thirty-five minutes, until nice and golden-brown.

Serve.

## Cajun Salmon

Serving Size: 1
Preparation Time: 10 minutes
Nutritional Information: 375 calories

INGREDIENTS

1 salmon fillet
Cajun seasoning
A light sprinkle of sugar
Juice from a quarter of lemon, to serve

INSTRUCTIONS

Preheat air fryer to 180 degrees. In a plate, sprinkle Cajun seasoning all over and ensure all sides are coated. You don't need too much. If you prefer a tad of sweetness, add a light sprinkling of sugar.

For a salmon fillet, about 3/4 of an inch thick, air fry for 7 minutes, skin side up on the grill pan. Serve immediately with a squeeze of lemon.

# French Toast Sticks

Serving Size: 2
Preparation Time: 10 minutes
Nutritional Information: 275 calories

INGREDIENTS

1 tbsp cinnamon
¼ tbsp nutmeg
¼ tbsp ground cloves
Maple Syrup to serve
4 slices of bread
2 tbsp approximately of soft butter
2 eggs gently beaten
1 tbsp salt

INSTRUCTIONS

Start off by preheating your Air fryer to approximately 180 degrees. Now put your eggs into a separate basket and gently beat together the eggs, ground cloves, some cinnamon, a sprinkle of salt, and few light dashes of nutmeg.

Cut the slices into thicker-sized strips and put butter on the strips. Dip each of your strips into the egg and place, delicately into the Air fryer. Make sure you leave enough space (you may have to cook a few different batches to cook all of them).

Air fry for about two minutes. Take the strips out of the frying pan and now you can place the pan on a heat-safe surface. Now, spray down the bread with the spray for cooking. Now that the strips have been coated, flip and spray the opposite sides as well. Put the Air fry pan back into the fryer and cook for 4 minutes. Make sure you are checking this every few minutes to ensure that it does not burn and cooks evenly all around.

When your egg has cooked and the bread strips are golden brown, you can now remove the strips from Air fryer. Now you may serve, immediately.

Enjoy!

## Sticky BBQ Pork Strips

Serving Size: 2
Preparation Time: 1 day
Nutritional Information: 275 calories

INGREDIENTS

2 tbsp Honey
1 tsp Balsamic Vinegar
¼ tsp Ground Ginger
6 packs Pork Chops (Loin)
2 tbsp Soy Sauce
Freshly Ground Pepper
1 clove Garlic

INSTRUCTIONS

Tenderize the pork loin chops with a tenderizer. Now season the loin chops with your freshly ground pepper. To prepare the marinade, soy sauce and honey into a bowl, pour the balsamic vinegar in the bowl as well. Add chopped garlic and ground ginger into the marinade. Make sure the mixture is well mixed and put away. Combine loin chops with the marinade and marinate it in a refrigerator overnight.
Preheat the air fryer at 180 degrees. Cook the chops in the air fryer tray along with your marinade for 8 to 10 minutes on each side until the chops are cooked completely and begin to turn light brown.
Cut the pork loin chops into strips or leave it alone as the full size chops. Enjoy!

# Coconut & Turmeric Chicken

Serving Size: 2
Preparation Time: 10 minutes
Nutritional Information: 275 calories

INGREDIENTS

3 whole chicken legs
50 grams coconut paste
5 tsp Ground Turmeric
50 grams Old Ginger
50 grams Galangal
¾ tbsp Salt

INSTRUCTIONS

Cut little slits in the leg of the chicken, making sure to not miss the thicker parts of the leg of the chicken. The slits are going to allow the chicken to take in more flavor. Mix chicken with your ingredients and leave it to marinate for at least four hours or overnight. Make sure that you wrap the chicken with saran wrap and put it into a cool place like a refrigerator.

Preheat the Air Fryer at 190 degrees. Air-fry the chicken for twenty to twenty-five minutes/

The chicken is ready when it turns into golden brown ball of delight.

# Fried Lemon Fish

Serving Size: 2
Preparation Time: 10 minutes
Nutritional Information: 300 calories

INGREDIENTS

2 tsp green chilli sauce
2 tsp oil
1 egg white
Salt to taste
1 tsp red chilli sauce
2-3 Lettuce leaves
4 tsp cornflour slurry
Juice of 1 lemon
¼ cup of sugar
4 pieces of fish fillets
Lemon 1

INSTRUCTIONS

Slice lemon and place in a bowl. Boil ½ cup water in a non-stick pan, add sugar and stir continuously till sugar dissolves. Put 1 cup refined flour, salt, green chilli sauce, 2 tsp oil and egg white in a bowl and make sure it's mixed well. Add 3 tbsp water and whisk well to create a thick and smooth mixture.

Spread sufficient refined flour on a plate. Dip the fish fillets in the batter and coat with refined flour. Heat an air fryer and brush the basket with oil. Place the prepared fish fillets in it, fit the basket to the fryer and cook at 180 degrees for 10-15 minutes.
Add salt to the pan with the syrup and mix well. Add cornflour slurry and mix again. Add red chilli sauce and mix well. Add lemon slices, lemon juice and mix well. Cook till the lemon sauce thickens.

Remove the fish from air fryer basket, brush with some oil and place in the air-fryer basket again. Continue to cook for 5 minutes more.

Roughly tear lettuce leaves and make a bed on a serving platter. Place fish over the lettuce, pour lemon sauce over them. Serve.

## Spicy Tuna Crispy Rice Sushi

Serving Size: 2
Preparation Time: 10 minutes
Nutritional Information: 275 calories

INGREDIENTS

2 green onions
4 cups of cooked rice
1 tsp of sugar
3 tbsp of rice vinegar
1 tsp of sriracha sauce
Olive oil spray
150 grams of sashimi tuna

INSTRUCTIONS

To make your sushi rice you will need to mix the vinegar with sugar and add to your rice. Make sure to mix this concoction. Cut tuna into small little chunks. The topping will be created by adding soy sauce and sriracha sauce into it. Mix fish completely until great texture.

Put your rice into the plastic wrap and bamboo roll and roll until it creates a log. Cut the log into sushi chunks of desired thickness. Place your rolls into the air fry nigiri rice for thirteen minutes in two-hundred degrees. Serve.

# Salmon Patties

Serving Size: 2
Preparation Time: 30 minutes
Nutritional Information: 310 calories

INGREDIENTS

Salt to taste
Breadcrumbs
Olive oil spray
A handful of parboiled frozen vegetables
3 large cooked russet potatoes
1 salmon portion
Chopped parsley
2 sprinkles of dill
Black pepper
1 egg

INSTRUCTIONS

Peel, chop, and mash cooked potatoes. Put this mixture to the side for later. Preheat for 5 minutes at one-hundred eighty degrees, then grill salmon for five minutes. Air fry the salmon. Perform an action called "flaking" which means to cut the salmon into smaller pieces with a fork. Set aside for later.

Remove your mashed potatoes from the refrigerator. Now you will add your vegetables, black pepper, chopped parsley, flaked salmon, and dill/salt. Do a taste test since everything is already cooked, and adjust seasonings to your liking. Add the egg and combine everything together.

Shape the mixture into six to eight patties or smaller balls. Cover the balls with breadcrumbs. Now make sure you spray oil onto the balls to keep them from sticking and breaking, and cook in air fryer at 180 degrees until golden brown. Serve!

# Honey lime chicken wings

Serving Size: 2
Preparation Time: 7 hours
Nutritional Information: 300 calories

INGREDIENTS

16 winglets
½ tsp sea salt
2 tbsp light soya sauce
¼ tsp white pepper powder
½ crush black pepper
2 tbsp honey
2 tbsp lime juice

INSTRUCTIONS

Pour all ingredients (except winglets) into a glass dish, add in mid wings, mix well and let it marinate for at least 6 hours if you don't have time. Cover with lip and refrigerate them.

Bring out to rest in room temperature for 30 mins. Air fry the wings with 180 degrees for 6 mins, flip over for another 6 mins.

Let it cool for 5 mins, serve with a wedge of lemon.

# Tiger Shrimp and Glass Noodle Salad

Serving Size: 6
Preparation Time: 30 minutes
Nutritional Information: 400 calories

INGREDIENTS

2 tsp piment d'espelette
2 tbsp evoo (oil)
Grated zest of 1 lime
Salt and freshly ground pepper
Grated zest of 1 lemon
18 large tiger shrimp, deveined and butterflied, tails intact
½ lb glass noodles, prepared according to the package instructions, drained and chilled
1 English cucumber, peeled, seeded and sliced on the diagonal
4 baby yellow bell peppers, seeded and thinly sliced
4 baby red bell peppers
½ cup fresh cilantro leaves
1 carrot, peeled and julienned
2 cups diced, sliced, and made into a julien, green papaya
½ cup fresh mint leaves
2 tbs julienned fresh basil leaves
2 green onions (thinly sliced on the diagonal)

For the dressing:
¼ cup lemon juice
½ cup soy sauce
2 tsp. Honey
thinly sliced 1 tbsp sweet chili sauce
1 cup grape seed oil
2 inch piece of fresh ginger

INSTRUCTIONS

Preheat a Philips Air fryer to 390 degrees. Stir together the piment d'Espelette and the 2 Tbs. olive oil. Make that mixture in a separate bowl. Now set them aside. Arrange the shrimp on a baking sheet and brush with the piment d'Espelette mixture.

Sprinkle the shrimp with the lemon and lime zests and season with salt and pepper.

Place 6 shrimp in the fry basket, cut side down, and insert into the air fryer. Cook for 4 minutes. Transfer to a baking sheet to cool. Repeat process.

Dressing: In a bowl, whisk together the lemon juice, honey, soy sauce, ginger, green onion and chili sauce. Slowly whisk in the oil until liquified.

Assemble the salad in a large bowl: toss the glass noodles, cucumber, bell peppers, carrot, green onions, papaya, mint and cilantro to combine. Add the vinaigrette to taste and toss everything in order to combine the mixture. Taste and adjust the seasoning if necessary. Divide the salad among 6 plates. Place 3 shrimps on top of each serving. Sprinkle with peanuts and basil. Serve.

## Cheesy Garlic Bread

Serving Size: 2
Preparation Time: 15 minutes
Nutritional Information: 200 calories

INGREDIENTS

5 round bread slices
4 tsp melted butter
3 chopped garlic cloves
5 tsp sun dried tomato pesto
1 cup grated mozzarella cheese

INSTRUCTIONS

As I am using baguette bread for my preparation, I will first cut it into thick round slices. Apply some melted butter (in which garlic cloves were added) on the bread slices. Apply a teaspoon of sun dried tomato pesto to each of the slice. Add a generous amount of grated cheese on the top of each slice.

Place these bread slices in air fryer and cook them at 180 degrees for 6-8 minutes. Garnish with some more freshly chopped basil leaves, chilli flakes and oregano!! Enjoy yummy cheesy garlic bread with ketchup as snack or appetizer.

## Kurkuri Bhindi/Okra

Serving Size: 2
Preparation Time: 20 minutes
Nutritional Information: 200 calories

INGREDIENTS

9 oz Bhindi/Okra/Ladyfinger
2 tsp gram flour
1 tsp red chilli
1 tsp coriander
½ tsp cumin
2 tsp mango powder
1 tsp chaat masala
2 tsp oil
1 tsp salt

INSTRUCTIONS

Wash the bhindi under running water and let it dry for some time. Slit all the bhindi vertically in four pieces. Sprinkle gram flour, coriander powder, salt, red chilli powder, cumin powder, mango powder, chaat masala and oil over it. Mix it well such that all the spices and gram flour sticks to the bhindi.

Preheat the electric fryer for 5 minutes at 200 degrees. Once it is preheated, place the bhindi on the air fryer's mesh and cook it at 180 degrees for next 13-15 minutes. Take the air-fryer basket out and flip the bhindi pieces after 5 minutes intervals. It may cook any moment after 10 minutes so keep an eye on it after this time.

"Kurkuri Bhindi" is ready. Top it up some more chaat masala if you'd like.

## Seasoned Potato Wedges

Serving Size: 2
Preparation Time: 15 minutes
Nutritional Information: 200 calories

INGREDIENTS

1 tsp dried and crushed oregano
3 large potatoes
1 tsp salt
1 tsp black pepper
½ tsp red chilli flakes
2 tbsp cornflour
1 tsp olive oil

INSTRUCTIONS

Peel the potatoes and cut them into wedges. Dissolve 1 tsp of salt in a bowl containing approximately 2 cups of water. Soak the potatoes in salt water for 20 to 30 minutes. Dry the potato wedges on a kitchen towel so that all its moisture is removed.

Add all the potato wedges in a bowl. Add oil, cornflour, dried oregano and red chilli flakes to it. Mix well so that all the spices stick to the potatoes. Preheat the air fryer at 180 degree celsius.

Place the seasoned potato wedges in air-fryer's basket and let it cook for 15 minutes at 180 degree celsius. Pull the basket out and give a good shake every 5 minutes. You may also brush some oil while shaking or can increase the cooking time as per your preference of browning. Sprinkle salt over it at the end.

## Macaroni and Cheese Balls

Serving Size: 2
Preparation Time: 15 minutes
Nutritional Information: 200 calories

INGREDIENTS

2 cups leftover macaroni and cheese
⅓ cup cheddar cheese
1 ½ cup milk (whole)
2 eggs
¾ cup white flour
1 cup bread crumbs

INSTRUCTIONS
Mix the shredded cheese with the leftover mac and cheese. Set aside.

Place the bread crumbs in a bowl. Mix the egg, milk, and other wet ingredients together and put in a bowl. With a small ice cream scoop, make ping pong size balls from the mac and cheese mixture.

Roll the mac and cheese balls in the flour, then the egg mixture. Finally, roll in the bread crumbs. Place the mac and cheese balls in the Fry Basket. Cook for 10 minutes at 360 degrees. Plate and serve.

## Mozzarella Sticks

Serving Size: 1
Preparation Time: 15 minutes
Nutritional Information: 420 calories

INGREDIENTS

1 lb mozzarella cheese
2 eggs
3 tbsp milk (non-fat)
½ cup flour
1 cup bread crumbs

INSTRUCTIONS
Cut cheese into 3 x ½ inch sticks. Place breadcrumbs in a bowl. Place flour in a bowl. Mix the egg and milk together and put in a bowl. Dip cheese sticks in flour, then egg, and finally bread crumbs.
Lay breaded sticks on a cookie sheet. Freeze in freezer for 1-2 hours or until solid.
Place small batches of breaded sticks. Scroll to the French Fries Icon. Cook 12 minutes at 400 degrees. Plate and serve.

## Garlic Knots

Serving Size: 2
Preparation Time: 15 minutes
Nutritional Information: 200 calories

INGREDIENTS

½ cup olive oil
1 lb of frozen pizza crust
1 tsp sea salt
1 tsp fresh parsley
1 tbsp garlic
1 tbsp parmesan cheese (grated)
Marinara sauce to dip

INSTRUCTIONS

Roll the pizza dough out until 1 inch thick. Slice the dough lengthwise. About 3/4 inch apart. Roll the dough between your palm and countertop. Make a knot with the dough and repeat until all the dough is used. Add the spices, cheese and olive oil and mix together in a bowl. Roll the knots into the oil mixture and place into the Fry Basket. Cook 12 minutes at 360 degrees. Flip over half way through. Serve with marinara sauce.

# Stromboli

Serving Size: 2
Preparation Time: 15 minutes
Nutritional Information: 200 calories

INGREDIENTS

⅓ lb cooked ham (sliced)
3 cup cheddar cheese (shredded)
1 egg yolk
1 tbsp milk
12 ounce pizza crust
¾ cup mozzarella cheese (shredded)
3 ounce red bell peppers (roasted)

INSTRUCTIONS

Roll the dough out until 1/4 inch thick. Layer the ham, cheese and peppers on one side of the dough. Fold over to seal. Combine the egg and milk together. Now brush the dough. Put your delicious stromboli into the Fry Basket. Cook for 15 minutes at 360 degrees. Every 5 minutes, carefully flip stromboli over. Plate and serve.

## Beef Roll Up

Serving Size: 2
Preparation Time: 20 minutes
Nutritional Information: 400 calories

INGREDIENTS

2 pound beef flank steak
3 tsp pesto
1 tsp black pepper
6 slices of provolone cheese
3 ounce red bell peppers (roasted)
¾ cup baby spinach
1 tsp sea salt

INSTRUCTIONS

Spread the pesto evenly on the meat. Layer the cheese, roasted red peppers & spinach ¾ of the way down the meat. Roll up and secure with toothpicks. Season with sea salt and pepper. Cook for 14 minutes at 400 degrees. Half way through, rotate the meat.

Let rest 10 minutes. Cut, plate, and serve.

## Chicken Tenders

Serving Size: 2
Preparation Time: 15 minutes
Nutritional Information: 200 calories

INGREDIENTS

1 tsp olive oil
1 tsp sea salt
½ cup flour
1 cup panko
½ tsp black pepper
6 chicken tenders
3 large eggs

INSTRUCTIONS

Place the panko in a pan. Mix with olive oil. Place the flour in a pan. Mix the egg and milk into a bowl.
Drench the chicken tenders into the flour, then the egg, and then the panko mixture.
Place into the basket and repeat until done. Cook for 14 minutes at 400 degrees. Half-way through cooking, flip the tenders over.

## Beef Empanadas

Serving Size: 2
Preparation Time: 15 minutes
Nutritional Information: 200 calories

INGREDIENTS

2 cloves garlic (minced)
½ tsp cumin
1 mini onion (diced)
Black pepper
1 egg yolk
Sea salt
¼ cup tomato salsa
½ green pepper (diced small)
1 lbs ground beef
1 package empanada shells
1 tbsp olive oil

INSTRUCTIONS

Put the air fryer on high heat on a relatively high temperature. Add the oil and ground beef and cook until all the meat is browned. Discard any excess fat. Add your onions and garlic. Cover and cook for 4 minutes.

Add the other ingredients except the egg, milk and empanada shells. Cook for 10 minutes on low. Mix the egg and milk together to make an egg wash.

Place an empanada shell on the counter. Add some of the cooked meat on one half of the rolled dough. Brush the edges with your egg wash and fold over. Seal with a fork. Brush with egg wash and place into the fry basket. Repeat until all are done. Cook for 10 minutes at 350 degrees.

Plate and serve.

## Rib Eye Steak

Serving Size: 2
Preparation Time: 15 minutes
Nutritional Information: 200 calories

INGREDIENTS

2 lb rib eye steak
1 tbsp steak rub
1 tbsp olive oil

INSTRUCTIONS

Season the steak on both sides with rub and olive oil. Place steak in the basket for 14 minutes at 400 degrees.

After 7 minutes, flip the steak.

When timer is done, remove steak from the air fryer. Let rest for 10 minutes before slicing. Enjoy and serve!

## Roast Turkey Breast

Serving Size: 2
Preparation Time: 15 minutes
Nutritional Information: 200 calories

INGREDIENTS

1 tbsp black pepper
2 tbsp olive oil
8 lb turkey breast
2 tbsp sea salt

INSTRUCTIONS

Season the turkey and rub with olive oil. Place the turkey breast side down in the Fry Basket. Cook for 20 minutes at 360 degrees. After 20 minutes, turn the breast over. Test the turkey with a thermometer for proper doneness (165 degrees).

Let rest for 20 minutes before serving.

# Roasted Chicken with Herbs

Serving Size: 2
Preparation Time: 15 minutes
Nutritional Information: 200 calories

INGREDIENTS

2 tbsp olive oil
5 lb whole chicken
1 tsp black pepper
½ tsp thyme
1 tsp garlic powder
1 tsp sea salt
1 tsp onion powder

INSTRUCTIONS

Season the turkey and rub with olive oil. Let it sit at room temperature for 45 minutes before cooking. Place the chicken breast side down in the Fry Basket. Cook for 20 minutes at 360 degrees. When time runs out, carefully turn the chicken over. Scroll to the Chicken Icon. Cook for 20 minutes at 360 degrees. Test the chicken with a thermometer for proper doneness (165 degrees). Let rest for 20 minutes before serving.

## Shrimp Spring Rolls

Serving Size: 2
Preparation Time: 20 minutes
Nutritional Information: 175 calories

INGREDIENTS

1 clove garlic (minced)
½ lbs cooked shrimp (chopped)
½ lb shiitake mushrooms
8 ounce water chestnuts (diced)
2 cup cabbage (sliced)
1 tsp ginger, minced
3 scallions (chopped)
sea salt and pepper
2 tbsp grapeseed oil
6 spring roll wrappers
1 egg yolk
1 tbsp water

INSTRUCTIONS

Place a pan on the stove on high heat. Add 1tbsp grapeseed oil. Repeat with the shiitakes, ginger, garlic and scallions. Add all of the ingredients to a bowl except the spring roll wrappers, egg and water.

Make egg wash with egg yolk and water. Once the shrimp is cooled, assemble the spring rolls. Lightly squeeze and drain any excess water from shrimp.

On the counter place one spring roll wrapper and coat the edges with the egg wash. Place a couple tablespoons of shrimp on the top of the wrapper and roll up, folding in the sides as you go. Place each spring roll into the Fry Basket. Cook for 15 minutes at 360 degrees. Turn occasionally during cooking process. Serve.

## Blooming Onion

Serving Size: 2
Preparation Time: 3 hours
Nutritional Information: 200 calories

INGREDIENTS

¾ cup whole wheat flour
½ tsp cajun seasoning
½ tsp black pepper
¼ sea salt
1 tsp garlic powder
¾ cup panko
1 ½ tsp paprika
½ cup milk (nonfat)
2 eggs
1 white onion

INSTRUCTIONS

Mix breadcrumbs with olive oil & Cajun seasoning. In a separate dish, mix salt & pepper into the flour. In a bowl, mix milk with egg. Peel onion, cut off top. Place cut side down onto a cutting board.
Starting ½ inch from the root, cut downward, all the way to the cutting board. Repeat to make 4 evenly spaced cuts around the onion. Continue slicing between each section until you have made 8 cuts total.

Place sliced onion in ice water for at least two hours or possibly overnight. Remove from water, pat until dry. Open onion so petals are exposed. Beat eggs with 2 Tbsp. milk. Place onion on a tray or in a bowl.

Sprinkle onion generously with flour mixture. Make sure to get in between all petals. Turn onion upside down to remove excess flour. Using a ladle, ladle the egg mixture into every crevice. Lift up onion and turn to make sure excess egg drips off.

Sprinkle onion very generously with bread crumb mixture. Press into place. Place the blooming onion into the Fry Basket. Cook for 10 minutes at 360 degrees. Leave foil on. When timer is done, check crispness of the onion. Cook 5-10 more minutes to desired crispness.

When done, remove carefully and serve.

## Blackened Chicken

Serving Size: 2
Preparation Time: 20 minutes
Nutritional Information: 210 calories

INGREDIENTS

2 chicken breasts
3 tbsp cajun spice

INSTRUCTIONS

Season the chicken breast generously with the Cajun spice by dredging the breast in the Cajun spice on both sides. Place the chicken breast into the basket. Cook for 10 minutes. After the 10 minutes, displace the chicken from the fryer. Slice the chicken breast and place over your favorite salad or sandwich.

# Country Fried Steak

Serving Size: 2
Preparation Time: 30 minutes
Nutritional Information: 475 calories

INGREDIENTS

1 tsp salt
6 ounce ground sausage meat
1 cup panko
1 tsp pepper
2 tsp flour
1 tsp garlic powder
6 ounce sirloin steak-pounded thin
3 eggs, beaten
1 cup flour
1 tsp pepper
2 cup milk
1 tsp onion powder

INSTRUCTIONS

Season the panko with the spices. Dredge the steak in this order. Flour, egg, and seasoned panko. Place the breaded steak into the basket of the Power Air Fryer and close. Cook for 12 minutes at 375 degrees. Remove the steak and serve with mash potatoes and sausage gravy.

In a pan cook the sausage until well done. Drain fat, reserve 2 tbsp in the pan. Add in the flour to the pan with sausage, mix until all the flour is incorporated. Slowly mix in the milk. Stir over a med heat until the milk thickens. Season with pepper.

Cook for 3 minutes to cook out the flour.

## Fish Taco

Serving Size: 1
Preparation Time: 20 minutes
Nutritional Information: 150 calories

INGREDIENTS

1 cup coleslaw
½ cup salsa
10 ounce cod filet
½ cup guacamole
2 tsp cilantro chopped
1 lemon cut
1 cup tempura batter
1 cup panko
1 tsp white pepper
6 flour tortillas

INSTRUCTIONS

Cut the Cod filets into long 2 oz pieces, season with salt and pepper. Dip each piece of Cod into the tempura batter, then dredge in the panko. Place the breaded Cod into the basket of the Air Fryer and close. Cook for 10 minutes. Press the power button.

Halfway through the cooking cycle turn the fish sticks. Once the timer has elapsed remove the fish stick from the Air Fryer. Spread guacamole on a tortilla. Place 1 fish stick on tortilla, top with some coleslaw, salsa, and a squeeze of lemon. Top with chopped cilantro, fold and eat.

## Roast Pork Loin with Red Potatoes

Serving Size: 2
Preparation Time: 35 minutes
Nutritional Information: 410 calories

INGREDIENTS

½ tsp red pepper flakes
2 red potatoes large dice
½ tsp garlic powder
1 tsp salt
1 tsp pepper
1 tsp parsley
balsamic glaze
2 lb pork loin

INSTRUCTIONS

Sprinkle the seasonings over the pork loin, and potatoes. Place the pork loin, then the potatoes next to the pork in the basket. Cook for 25 minutes. After 25 minutes, remove the pork loin from the Air Fryer. Set aside for a few minutes before slicing. Plate the roasted potatoes. Slice the pork. Place 4-5 slices over the potatoes and drizzle the balsamic glaze over the pork. Serve.

# Pumpkin Spice Cannoli Pumpkin Patch

Serving Size: 2
Preparation Time: 15 minutes
Nutritional Information: 200 calories

INGREDIENTS

1 cup sugar
½ cup pumpkin pie mix
⅓ cup confectioners sugar
8 large flour tortillas
1 tbsp ground cinnamon
2 pound whole milk ricotta
4 tbsp butter (melted)
½ cup orange sanding sugar
½ cup mini chocolate chips

INSTRUCTIONS

Make the tortilla crisps. Use a pumpkin cookie cutter to cut out as many pumpkins as possible from the tortillas. Brush one side of the pumpkin cutouts with the melted butter. Sprinkle with orange sanding sugar. Mix together the cinnamon and sugar in a small bowl and stir to combine. Sprinkle the cinnamon and sugar mixture over the cookies. Cook the cookies, in batches, in the Air Fryer, set at 400 degrees for 3 minutes, until crisp.

Cool completely on cooling racks. Meanwhile, make the pumpkin spice cannoli dip. Now you can combine the ricotta, pumpkin pie mix and sugar. Stir to combine all ingredients.

Transfer the dip to a shallow platter. Arrange the pumpkin crisps in the dip to create a
pumpkin patch. Sprinkle with mini chocolate chips.

## Chicken and Rice

Serving Size: 1
Preparation Time: 30 minutes
Nutritional Information: 450 calories

INGREDIENTS

1 tsp cumin
1 tsp oregano
6 ounce white rice
1 tbsp tomato paste
8 ounce chicken stock
1 cup green and red pepper (diced)
¼ onion (diced)
½ cup tomato (diced)
1 tsp turmeric
1 pinch salt and pepper
6 ounce chicken thigh boneless meat

INSTRUCTIONS

Combine all ingredients into the Inner Pot. Mix. Place the lid on. Keep warm when the rice is finished cooking.

## Butternut Risotto

Serving Size: 2
Preparation Time: 10 minutes
Nutritional Information: 175 calories

INGREDIENTS
3 tbsp butter
2 tbsp olive oil
2 sage leaves
1 cup parmesan cheese
¼ cup heavy Cream
2 cup risotto
1 cinnamon stick
salt and pepper
1 cup chicken stock
1 ½ cup butternut squash
¼ cup white wine
1 small onion (diced)

INSTRUCTIONS

Cook onion/butternut squash and cook until tender. Mix together the cinnamon and sage, risotto, cook your mixture for about two of the minutes from a timer or other timekeeping device. Add the wine and cook until the risotto absorbs the wine. Repeat with the chicken stock in small amounts until all the stock is absorbed and risotto is tender and creamy. Add the cream, S&P and cheese mix. Serve

# Chapter 3: DESERTS

**Chocolate Steam Pudding**

Serving Size: 2
Preparation Time: 15 minutes
Nutritional Information: 200 calories
INGREDIENTS
½ cup Heavy Cream
6 ounce Melted dark chocolate
1 cup Chocolate chips, semi-sweet
1 tbsp Baking Powder
4 tsp Cocoa Powder
½ cup Butter, room temp.
¾ cup Brown Sugar
2 Eggs
1 tbsp Vanilla Extract
½ cup Heavy Cream
1 cup All purpose flour

INSTRUCTIONS

Mix together sugar and butter in a medium sized bowl. Add in one egg at a time to make sure the egg doesn't cook with the high energy. Continue to mix until the flour has been incorporated. Mix in the chocolate and the rest of your mixture.
Using non-stick spray, make sure the pudding pan does not stick. Place the pudding into the pudding pan and cover the pan with a lid to ensure freshness. Place the basket into the air fryer pot.
Pour 2 cups of warm water into the main pot of the cooker. Place the steam pudding pan into the inner pot.
Cook for 10 minutes. Carefully remove the pudding from the cooker and cool for 2 hours.
Bring to a boil, and add cream to the mix. Cancel the air fryer operation to allow heat to stop. Stir in the chocolate chip to create a very smooth and delightful glaze.
Pour the glaze over the chocolate steamed pudding.
Enjoy and serve!

# Cranberry Orange Bread Pudding

Serving Size: 2
Preparation Time: 15 minutes
Nutritional Information: 200 calories

INGREDIENTS

4 Egg yolks
2 cup Half & Half
1 Orange, zested and juiced
0.5 tbsp Vanilla
2 tsp Butter, Soft
0.75 cup Sugar
0.75 cup Cranberries
3 cup Brioche, cubed

INSTRUCTIONS

In a medium size bowl, mix the eggs, orange juice, sugar, cranberries, half & half, zest, and vanilla extract. Soak the cubed brioche in the egg for ten minutes.

Pour this concoction into a six-inch baking dish and cover the dish with foil or three smaller ramekins. Pour two cups of warmer than room temperature, water into the inner pot of the cooker. Place the baking dish on the rack in the cooker. Cook for fifteen minutes.

Now you can remove the Bread Pudding from the cooker and remove all of the foil from the pan. Serve after allowing to get room temperature.

## Pumpkin Cheesecake

Serving Size: 2
Preparation Time: 20 minutes
Nutritional Information: 200 calories

INGREDIENTS
0.5 cup cooked pumpkin
2 cups cream cheese
0.75 cup sugar
1 tablespoon cinnamon
2 eggs
0.5 tablespoon Vanilla Extract
1 cup graham cracker crust
0.25 cup sugar
2 tablespoons butter (melted)

INSTRUCTIONS

Mix together your sugar, graham cracker crumbs, and your butter. Put your crust in a six in. cheesecake baking plate and push down the crumbs to create a flattened crust at the bottom of your pan. Put the sugar and cream cheese in a bowl.

Use an electric mixer to mix. Add in one egg between each stir to ensure the egg doesn't cook from the high energy. Pour in the rest and mix together. Now pour your concoction into the cheesecake pan to create the filling.

Wrap the pan with foil, completely. Place the pot into the cooker. Pour a cup of lukewarm water into the inner pot. Now put the cheesecake pan into the cooker.

Once all of the steam has completely been released, you are able to remove the lid. Make sure to be careful when moving the lid from the cheesecake. You can now lift away the foil. Allow the cheesecake to cool down in the fridge for two hours. Once the cheesecake has begun to set and stiffen, remove from the pan. Serve and enjoy!

# Candied Yam and Marshmallow Hand Pies

Serving Size: 2
Preparation Time: 30 minutes
Nutritional Information: 355 calories

INGREDIENTS

16 ounce can of candied yams, syrup drained
0.5 teaspoon cinnamon
0.25 teaspoon allspice
0.25 teaspoon salt
1 crescent dough sheet
0.5 cup maple syrup
2 tablespoons marshmallow creme
1 egg, beaten
½ cup confectioners sugar

INSTRUCTIONS

Use a fork to smash the yams and stir to combine the spices. Place the crescent dough sheet on a cutting board. Cut into 4 equal pieces. Spread a generous mound of the yam filling in the center of 2 of the dough squares.

Top with a tablespoon of marshmallow creme. Brush the edges of the dough, using your pastry brush, with some egg wash. Top with the 2 remaining squares of dough. Use a fork to crimp the edges. Cut 3 slits on the top of the hand pie for venting. Transfer to the air fryer. Cook at 400 for 6 minutes.

Making the maple glaze will require you to put the confectioner's sugar into a small bowl. Add the maple syrup in small splashes before it is time for the sugar to become completely dissolved and the glaze slowly runs off a spoon. Drizzle the glaze over the warm hand pies.

# Luxury 10 Minute Chocolate Profiteroles

Serving Size: 3-4
Preparation Time: 15 minutes
Nutritional Information: 200 calories

INGREDIENTS

Profiteroles:
3.5 oz Butter
7 oz Plain Flour
6 Medium Eggs
½ cup Water
Cream Filling:
2 tsp Vanilla Essence
2 tsp Icing Sugar
⅓ cup Whipped Cream

Chocolate Sauce:
3.5 oz milk Chocolate (broken into chunks)
2 tbsp Whipped Cream
½ stick Butter

INSTRUCTIONS

Preheat the air fryer to 170 degrees. Place the fat in the water in a large pan and cook on a medium heat and make sure you bring it to the boil. Remove it from the heat and stir in the flour (a bit at a time) and then put it back on the heat until it forms a big dough in the middle of the pan. Set the dough to one side so that it can cool down. Mix together and continue to add the eggs into the mixture well until you have a smooth mixture.

Make into profiterole shapes and cook for 10 minutes on 180 degrees. While the éclairs are cooking make the cream filling – mix with a whisk vanilla essence, whipped cream and icing sugar until nice and thick. While the profiteroles are cooking make the chocolate topping – place the chocolate, butter and cream in a glass bowl, over a pan of boiling water. Mix well until you have melted chocolate.
Finish your profiteroles with melted chocolate on top.

# Stuffed Sweet Mushrooms with Sour Cream

Serving Size: 3-4
Preparation Time: 15 minutes
Nutritional Information: 200 calories

INGREDIENTS

24 medium size mushrooms, stalks removed
1/2 capsicum
One cup grated cheese
1/2 cup sour cream
1 small carrot
extra cheese, for the top
2 rashers bacon
1/2 onion

INSTRUCTIONS

Finely dice the bacon, onion, capsicum, carrots and mushroom stalks.
Saute the diced bacon and vegetables in a fry pan until all are soft. Stir in the sour cream and cheese then continue to heat until the cheese has melted and all have combined well. Add the stuffing in a heaped fashion to each and sprinkle with a little cheese.

Preheat the air fryer to 180 degrees. Add the mushrooms and cook for eight minutes.

# Cinnamon and Sugar Doughnuts

Serving Size: 4
Preparation Time: 15 minutes
Nutritional Information: 175 calories

INGREDIENTS

Doughnuts:
1 teaspoon salt
2 large egg yolks
50 grams butter (melted)
1/2 cup sour cream

Cinnamon Sugar:
1/3 cup caster sugar
2 tablespoons butter
1/2 cup sugar
1 teaspoon cinnamon
2 1/4 cup plain flour
1 1/2 teaspoons baking powder

INSTRUCTIONS

The sugar and butter needs to be mixed until it becomes crumbly. Now, add your egg yolks from the egg and stir until fully mixed. Make sure you sift your flour, salt and baking powder into your bowl designated for dry ingredients. Add half of the sour cream and a third of the flour.

When well combined add another ½ of the sour cream and ⅓ of the flour. Now you can add in and mix the sour cream to the concoction. Place the mixture in the refrigerator while you work on the other ingredients. Lightly flour the bench then roll-out the dough about 1 centimeter of thickness. Cut large circles, then a small circle out the centre to create a doughnut shape.

Preheat your air fryer to one-hundred eighty degrees. Now, with a brush, use the melted butter, place thin layers of the butter on each side of the donut and add it to the air fryer for frying. Cook for eight minutes.

As soon as the doughnuts are cooked, paint again with the melted butter and immediately dip into the cinnamon sugar mixture. Serve and eat hot. Like traditional doughnuts they are much better hot than cold.

# Chocolate Cake

## Serving Size: 2

Preparation Time: 1 hour
Nutritional Information: 400 calories

INGREDIENTS

1,8 oz caster sugar
1,8 oz butter
1 egg
1 tablespoon apricot jam
1,8 oz plain flour
1 tablespoon cocoa
salt, to taste
icing sugar, to present

INSTRUCTIONS

Preheat the air fryer to 160 degrees. Spray a small ring cake tin with your spray designated for non-stick purposes.

Now you can mix the sugar with the softened butter until creamy and light. Add the egg and jam then combine into the butter.

Sift in the salt, cocoa powder, and flour. Mix thoroughly. Transfer your batter to the ring tin and use the back of a fork to level the surface.

Place your cake tin in the air-fryer basket. Set the timer to 15 minutes and bake the cake until you can insert a toothpick into the centre of the cake and it comes out very cleanly.

## Banana Cake

Serving Size: 3
Preparation Time: 1 hour
Nutritional Information: 300 calories

INGREDIENTS

1,8 oz butter, at room temperature
1 egg
1/3 cup brown sugar
1 cup flour
2 tablespoons honey
1/2 teaspoon cinnamon
pinch salt, to taste
1 banana, mashed

INSTRUCTIONS

Preheat your air fryer to 160 degrees. Use non-stick spray to create a non-stick surface for your small ring-cake tin. In a bowl beat the sugar with the butter until creamy.

Add the egg, banana and honey then whisk into the butter mixture until smooth. Sift in the flour, salt, and cinnamon then mix to make the cake batter.

Transfer the batter to the ring tin and use the back of a spoon to level the surface. Put the cake tin in the air fryer basket.

Set the timer to 30 minutes and bake the cake until a fork, when inserted in the centre that is the thicke of the cake is extracted cleanly.

## Apple Dumplings

Serving Size: 3
Preparation Time: 1 hour
Nutritional Information: 225 calories

INGREDIENTS

2 very small apples
2 tablespoons sultanas
1 tablespoon brown sugar
2 sheets puff pastry
2 tablespoons butter, melted

INSTRUCTIONS

Preheat your air fryer to 180 degrees. Core and peel the apples. Mix the sultanas and the brown sugar.
Put each apple on one of the puff pastry sheets then fill the core with the sultanas and sugar. Fold the pastry around the apple so it is fully covered.

Place the apple dumplings on a small sheet of foil (so if any juices escape they don't fall into the air fryer). Brush the dough with the melted butter.

Place in you air fryer for 25 minutes and bake the apple dumplings until golden brown and the apples are soft.

## Pineapple Sticks with Yogurt Dip

Serving Size: 3
Preparation Time: 1 hour
Nutritional Information: 225 calories

INGREDIENTS

Pineapple Sticks
1/2 pineapple
1/4 cup desiccated coconut
Yogurt Dip
1 small sprig fresh mint
1 cup vanilla yogurt

INSTRUCTIONS

Pineapple Sticks: Preheat your air fryer to 200 degrees. Cut the pineapple into sticks, similar size and shape to chips.

Dip the pineapple into desiccated coconut, the moisture in the pineapple is enough to make it stick. Gently lay the pineapple sticks into the basket and cook for 10 minutes

Yogurt Dip: Finely dice the mint leaves then stir through the vanilla yogurt.

Plate and serve.

## Fruit Crisp

Serving Size: 3
Preparation Time: 1 hour
Nutritional Information: 225 calories

INGREDIENTS

Soft shell tortillas (traditional ones and not low carb)
raspberries
blueberries
strawberry jelly
powdered sugar

INSTRUCTIONS

Preheat your air fryer to 300 degrees. Lay out the desired number of tortillas. One tortilla serves 1-2 people. Layer a thin layer of jelly on top of each tortilla. Top with scattered blueberries and raspberries. Dust with powdered sugar.

Carefully pick up your fruit crisp by the edges and lay it gently in the Air Fryer pan. Cook the crisp for about five minutes until the edges are lightly golden.

When finished cooking, pull the pan out and use a spatula while tilting the pan on its side to carefully remove the crisp onto a plate. Top with a little extra powdered sugar and roll tortilla in half to make a fruit taco. You can also cut it into slices to make a fruit pizza.

# Holiday Cake

Serving Size: 2
Preparation Time: 1 hour
Nutritional Information: 445 calories

INGREDIENTS
2½ cups all-purpose flour
1 cup milk
¾ cup butter
¼ teaspoon salt
3 eggs
3 teaspoons baking powder
Red + Green Icing
1 teaspoon vanilla
White Frosting
1¼ cups sugar

INSTRUCTIONS

Grease the bottom of two eight inch round pans. Mix salt, baking powder, and sifted flour in one bowl. Mix together the butter and sugar with an electric mixer or other appliance that accomplishes the same task. Add the vanilla and eggs mixture to the sugar concoction and beat the entire concoction until fully mixed.

Add the milk and sugar mixture to the flour mixture, making sure to beat the mixture well after adding each ingredient until it is all completely mixed together.

Divide the cake batter, creating two separate portions. Use a toothpick to add the color, green for one and red for the other. Put your first cake in the Air fryer and bake for twenty to twenty-four minutes.

Place your second cake in the Air fryer and bake for twenty to twenty-four minutes or until your toothpick comes out clean.

## Almost Famous Chocolate Cake

Serving Size: 2
Preparation Time: 1 hour
Nutritional Information: 400 calories

INGREDIENTS

1 large egg
1/4 cup vegetable oil
2 cup milk
1 tsp vanilla extract
1/2 tsp salt
1/2 cup hot water (add in some instant coffee powder)
6 oz Brown Sugar or 12 tablespoons
3/4 tsp baking soda
109 g all purpose flour or 7 tablespoons
2 oz unsweetened cocoa powder or 4 tablespoons
3/4 tsp baking powder

INSTRUCTIONS

Preheat the Air-fryer at one-hundred eighty degrees for 5 minutes. Mix all your dry ingredients. Add in the milk, vanilla extract, egg, and oil to the dry mixture. Gently stir the concoction to mix it even and well. Lastly, add your hot water. Again, gently stir it to make sure the mixture is mixed evenly.

Pour this concoction into your baking pan and cover the baking with some foil and stab some breathing holes into it. Put your baking tray in the air fryer basket. Air Bake for thirty-five minutes. Remove the foil that you placed on the cake and continue baking the cake for another ten minutes until the skewer comes out clean.

Be sure to let it chill in the pan for about ten minutes before removing the cake from the pan. Let your cake chill before removing it from the air fry as it might fall apart. Plate and serve!

# Thai Style Fried Bananas

Serving Size: 1
Preparation Time: 1 hour
Nutritional Information: 400 calories

INGREDIENTS

a pinch of salt
2 tablespoon rice flour
2 tablespoon corn flour
½ tsp cardamom powder
¼ cup more rice flour for coating
4 bananas (ripe)
2 tbsp maida
2 tbsp desiccated coconut
½ tsp baking powder
Some oil for drizzling
¼ sesame seeds for the outer covering

INSTRUCTIONS

To start cooking this delicious Fried Bananas recipe, gather your many ingredients and make sure to hold them near by you. You should begin by making the lovely mixture for the fried bananas. Into a large bowl, add in rice flour, the maida, corn flour, salt, baking powder, coconut and stir to mix well.

Next add in bits of water over time in order to create a thick and very smooth mixture. The batter should be such that it can coat the back of a spoon. Have your sesame seeds and rice flour handy.

If you are using small bananas (as big as your thumb sometimes), then slice these lengthwise into a nice half banana.

Next butter up a 8 x 8 inch foil or use butter paper with a bit of oil. This is important so that we don't get fried bananas that stick to our tray. The butter and flour will act as a non-stick agent in this portion of the recipe. Cover up and trim the foil or the butter paper, making sure to pinch the ends so as to leave a little break for proper air circulation.

Dip banana slices into your batter and then roll the banana slices into your sesame seeds and rice flour.

You can add sesame seeds to the top for an added crunchiness to the dish. Put your bananas that have been dipped into the batter into the greased foil or butter paper.

Now you can air fry the bananas at 200 degrees for about 10 to 15 minutes, flipping half way through so it gets fried evenly all around. Serve and enjoy!

## Sponge Cake

Serving Size: 1
Preparation Time: 1 hour
Nutritional Information: 400 calories

INGREDIENTS

2 tsp evoo (oil)
¼ tsp lemon extract
3 eggs
¼ cup raw sugar
Zest of 1 lime
Pinch salt
½ cup plain flour
1 tsp baking powder
1 tbsp milk (2%)
1 tsp pure vanilla (extract)

INSTRUCTIONS

Heat your air fryer to 180 degrees. Line a seven inch, round cake tin with parchment baking paper. Sift the salt, flour, and baking powder. Put aside. Mix your powdered sugar with eggs, lemon extract, and vanilla in a large bowl over a pan of water for about seven minutes.

Now begin to add the flour mix. Fold the mix to ensure proper mixing. Now add the milk and olive oil. Transfer batter to a prepared tin and bake for fifteen minutes in the air fryer until light golden brown. Allow to cool for about 5 minutes. Now, demold and chill completely on cooling rack. Plate and serve.

# Banana Walnuts and Oats Muffin

Serving Size: 1
Preparation Time: 1 hour
Nutritional Information: 210 calories

INGREDIENTS

¼ cup unsalted butter/ ghee
¼ cup powdered sugar
1 tsp milk
¼ cups oats
¼ cups of mashed banana
½ tsp baking powder
4 tbsp refined flour (maida)
1 tsp walnuts – 1 tsp (chopped)

INSTRUCTIONS

Mix butter and sugar together and add mashed banana and walnuts. In separate bowl, mix flour, oats and baking powder. Add these dry ingredients in the above mixture and cut and fold the mixture 3-4 times. Add little milk if the batter seems to be very thick. Grease muffin mould and put the muffin batter in each mould.

Some walnuts can be put on top of each mould as well. Bake the muffins in preheated air fryer at 160 degrees for 10 min. Once baked, keep muffins in standby time for another 10 min. Take out muffin mould and allow to cool for 10 minutes. Plate muffins and serve.

## Molten Lava Cakes

Serving Size: 1
Preparation Time: 1 hour
Nutritional Information: 300 calories

INGREDIENTS

3 ½ ounce unsalted butter
3 ½ ounce dark chocolate
2 eggs
1 ½ tbsp flour (self-rising)
3 ½ tbsp baker's sugar

INSTRUCTIONS

Grease and flour 4 standard oven safe ramekins. Melt dark butter and chocolate in a microwave safe bowl on level 7 for 3 minutes, stirring throughout. Remove from microwave and stir until even consistency. Whisk/Beat the eggs and sugar until pale and frothy.

Pour melted chocolate mixture into egg mixture. Stir in flour. Use a spatula to combine everything evenly. Fill small white ramekins about three-quarters of the way full with cake mixture and bake in air fryer at 375 degrees for ten minutes.

Remove from the air fryer and make sure they cool for about 2 minutes. Carefully turn ramekins upside down onto serving plate, tapping the bottom with a butter knife to loosen edges. Plate and serve.

# Lemon Sponge Gateau

Serving Size: 1
Preparation Time: 1 hour
Nutritional Information: 200 calories

INGREDIENTS

8 oz butter – room temperature
1 tsp grated lemon zest
1 tsp baking powder
8 oz self raising flour
8 oz caster sugar
2 eggs

INSTRUCTIONS

Make sure to preheat your Air Fryer to 160 degrees to make sure it gets going before you start working on the gateau batter. Prepare the baking tins that you will be using by spraying them with butter.

Combine all of your ingredients into a bowl and double check, making sure the mix is viscous and well-mixed. This should make about two different cakes for you using a standard air fryer.

Bake the cake for fifteen minutes in your air fryer. Wait until the cook is a light sand color and soft. Remove tin out of the Air Fryer, move away from the pan and make sure it cools. Now repeat the whole process with the other bit of the batter.

Plate and serve.

## Lemon Candy Treats

Serving Size: 1
Preparation Time: 30 minutes
Nutritional Information: 20 calories

INGREDIENTS

2 organic lemons
½ cup sugar
1 cup boiling water

INSTRUCTIONS

Start this off by making a delicious sugar reduction syrup, now add in boiling water to a bowl with your sugar inside of it. Stir the mixture to make sure that all of the sugar is finely dissolved. Place sugar syrup next to you in case you are ready for it.

Slice your lemons into very thin slices. After you have sliced your lemons, dip the lemons into your sugar syrup mixture and put them on a flat baking sheet.

Bake the lemons in the air fryer, allowing them to dry out and become chewable as well. Make sure your air fryer is set to 120 degrees for about thirty to forty minutes or until lemons are slightly chewy and sticky.

## Striped Butter Cake

Serving Size: 4
Preparation Time: 45 minutes
Nutritional Information: 225 calories

INGREDIENTS

1 cup milk
1 stick of butter
3,5 oz flour (self-rising and sifted)
1 tsp vanilla extract
2 eggs
3,5 oz castor sugar
1 tbsp of cocoa powder

INSTRUCTIONS

Grease the inside of a 6" baking tin that has been lined with parchment paper. Create a fluffy sugar and butter. Add your eggs into the mixture one at a time, and then add milk and vanilla mixture. Mix well in mixer. Add sifted flour and mix till incorporated. Scoop half batter out and set aside. Add cocoa powder to the batter in mixer and mix well.

Scoop 2 tbsp of the plain batter on center of baking tin. Then scoop 2 tbsp of chocolate batter on the centre of the plain batter in the baking tin. Continue to scoop.

Place baking tin in air fryer and cook at 160 for about 30 minutes. Serve and enjoy!

# Conclusion

Thank you for downloading this book!

Hopefully this book gave you some really great tips and ideas for cooking amazingly fancy cuisine using your air fryer.

The sheer variety of meals that one can cook with the air fryer makes it a necessary component in any one's kitchen. Throw out all of those pots, pans, and fattening oils and trade them in for your very own air fryer.

Thank you again and happy eating!

Printed in Great Britain
by Amazon